WINFIELD SCOTT

A Biography of Scottsdale's Founder

An Official
Arizona Bicentennial Commemorative Publication

Winfield Scott
1837–1910

WINFIELD SCOTT

A Biography of Scottsdale's Founder

by

RICHARD E. LYNCH

Published by

The City of Scottsdale

Arizona

Contents

Illustrations

Foreword

Every community should assume the obligation to capture its past, and I am pleased that during my mayoralty Scottsdale has begun this task with its support of Richard Lynch's splendid biography of Chaplain Winfield Scott, our city's founder.

Unlike many other romantic western communities, Scottsdale did not wither away. Instead it sustained a gradual process of growth and development. While Tombstone was labeled "the town too tough to die," Scottsdale, by the same token, may be said to have matured gracefully like a beautiful lady. Maturing gracefully in itself is a process which takes forethought and planning in order to cultivate those qualities which are most enduring. It was this task that Chaplain Scott set for himself when he arrived in the Salt River Valley in the late 1880s.

The work that Winfield Scott undertook here not only insured his role in history, but it also initiated a way of life and provided a foundation for the people who would follow and call Scottsdale home. Winfield Scott was a solid builder, not a get-rich-quick promoter. He devoted his energies to the development of an agricultural base for the tiny community, one which would provide the foundation for sound economic and social evolution.

Scottsdale many years later would pride itself on a democratic institution termed "community involvement." Perhaps it took its lead in this regard from the life which emanated from the Scott ranch. The ranch served as the focal point for all manner of community gatherings, from special holidays to simple neighborhood get-togethers. While these were intended to be primarily social in nature, undoubtedly many dreams for the future of this desert oasis were spun out by those in attendance. And, in the final analysis, that is what makes communities vital and progressive, people who have dreams and can see beyond the present crises to a better tomorrow.

The members of the Scottsdale City Council are pleased to have been a part of this worthy project. It is of importance to any modern city to know not only where it is trying to go but also where it has been. Scottsdale is still a young town. The day when Chaplain Scott began unfolding his dreams was not too long ago. There are still those in the community who can remember the days of the Scott family, and they have gladly shared with Dick Lynch their fond memories and treasured keepsakes from the past. In capturing the history of one man and his life's work, he has unfolded the early story of the community which grew to mean so much to that Christian man of the frontier. Drawing upon heretofore untapped community and national resources, he has pieced together an account of Scottsdale in its infancy. In a later book he will relate the story of its emergence as a modern center of 20th century sophistication. To tie these chapters in Scottsdale's life together has been for the author not only a professional accomplishment but clearly a labor of love as well. As this young historian has told us of the past, we can only hope that those of us who now have a hand in shaping the destiny of this community will not be untrue to the vision of Chaplain Scott, soldier, farmer, community leader, and man of God.

William C. Jenkins
Mayor

November, 1977

Preface

This book tells the story of Army Chaplain Winfield Scott, the founding father of Scottsdale, Arizona. It is the story of a dynamic and restless man and the part he played in the development of the American West from the end of the Civil War through the first decade of the twentieth century. Until now, many who have heard the name Winfield Scott associated with the founding of Scottsdale have confused the chaplain with the famous general of the same name who served with distinction in the Mexican War of 1846–1848. One of the main purposes of this book, then, is to make Scott's story known in order to dispel the confusion. "Old Fuss and Feathers" did not found Scottsdale; a measurably more interesting man with the same name has that distinction, and it is time to set the record straight.

Ironically, there is an uncorroborated story which links the two Winfield Scotts, and it begins with three Scott brothers leaving the British Isles at the beginning of the eighteenth century to seek their fortunes in the New World. One brother settled in Connecticut, another in New Jersey, and the third found his way to Virginia. We know that the Connecticut Scotts sired the Winfield Scott of Scottsdale history, and, according to the story, the Virginia branch of the family sired the famous general. Whether or not the story is factual remains to be proved, but Scottsdale's founder believed himself to be a distant cousin of the Virginia soldier, and since he believed in the connection, I have chosen to include the story here.

Research for this book began in the summer of 1974, when I was hired to implement an oral history project established by the Scottsdale-Paradise Valley Bicentennial Commission to gather and preserve the history of the Scottsdale-Paradise Valley area. In active support of the commission, the City of Scottsdale secured funding for the project through a summer grant from the Western Interstate Commission on Higher Education.

In seeking a starting point for Scottsdale-Paradise Valley history, I consulted many "old-timers," read magazine articles on Scottsdale history, and waded into Bert Fireman's newspaper archives at Arizona State University. It soon became clear that Winfield Scott had not only begun the civilizing process in the area, but that he had also distinguished himself throughout his career, long before coming to the Salt River Valley. Armed with a series of newspaper references and clues provided by people who had known Scott, I began an extensive correspondence with historical societies, museums, libraries, and individuals in the many towns where Winfield Scott had lived. The material I received in answer to my inquiries, combined with additional material from Arizona sources, convinced me that Scott deserved the lion's share of the project's time and resources. His career exemplified the spirit which the Bicentennial planners hoped to capture and perpetuate.

Both the Bicentennial Commission and the City of Scottsdale agreed to a major shift in the project's emphasis, and the biography of Chaplain Winfield Scott became the primary goal. While I continued to conduct interviews, ferret out old photographs, and search various Arizona archives for Scottsdale material, Chaplain Scott became the focus of my attention.

At the end of the summer of 1974, in order that the project might continue, the City of Scottsdale hired me as a part-time city employee. A generous grant from the Arizona Bicentennial Commission also greatly assisted in the completion of this book. The grant allowed the project to purchase invaluable archival material which would have been otherwise unavailable, to hire a part-time research assistant, and to provide me with essential trips to the Bancroft Library at the University of California, Berkeley; to the Western History Department of the Denver Public Library; and to Calexico, California, to interview a captivating lady who knew Chaplain Scott when she was a young girl. In addition, the members of the Scottsdale City Council, Mayor William C. Jenkins, the city staff, Mary King, the Scottsdale Historical Society, and many citizens of Scottsdale have been extremely helpful in seeing this project to completion. Furthermore, the City of Scottsdale has given me complete academic freedom in the writing of this book. If I have presented Winfield Scott in a favorable light, it is because I have developed a positive Scott bias and not because I have been asked to provide positive coloring.

During the course of my research I uncovered relatively little negative material concerning Scott, and that which could be substantiated has been included in this book. Perhaps his personal papers, all of which burned in a fire in 1895, would have revealed more, but the public record exhibits little of a derogatory nature. Having lived with this remarkable man for the past three years, I have developed a genuine respect and affection for him, and the reader should be aware of that fact in reading this biography. My favorable bent toward the chaplain is honestly come by and openly admitted.

In leafing through the book, the reader will note that there are few source notes for each chapter and that those notes cite only secondary sources. This has been done purposefully in the interests of economy and with the intent of interfering as little as possible with the flow of the narrative. Anyone interested in studying the many primary source citations can do so by consulting my master's thesis which can be found in the Charles Trumbull Hayden Library at Arizona State University. A complete bibliography has been provided, however, to give the reader an idea of the sources used to reconstruct the life of Winfield Scott.

The Scottsdale City Council, in an unusual gesture of civic pride and community consciousness in these times of tight municipal budgets, has seen fit to continue the original oral history project. As a result, oral interviews and primary historical research have continued apace, and a companion volume on the history of Scottsdale is scheduled for future publication.

It seems genuinely appropriate that this book, which was begun as an official Bicentennial project, should owe so much to so many people. The cooperation and assistance from individuals and institutions all across this country have been remarkable and in the best Bicentennial spirit. In this regard, the Scottsdale-Paradise Valley Bicentennial Commission must be singled out at the beginning for its vision in initiating this project. Without the foresight, interest, and enthusiasm of its members the Winfield Scott biography would not have seen the light of day. I must especially thank Roberta Unterberger, president of the commission; Richard Kiesell, treasurer; and William W. Phillips, heritage committee chairman, for their unflaging support and encouragement. They gave a great deal of their time, energy, and good offices to see that the project came to a successful conclusion. The Arizona Bicentennial Commission; its executive director, Maurice M. Giss; its chairmen, the late John H. Eversole, Dr. John R. Carney, and Felix L. Goodwin; and most especially its representative from Scottsdale, Maxine Marshall, also deserve a sincere vote of thanks for both their monetary and moral support. The state commission had a multitude of projects competing for its limited resources, and the grant it tendered to the Scott project was much appreciated. I am most indebted, however, to Mayor

William C. Jenkins and the Scottsdale City Council. Without their commitment, this book could not have been completed.

I also owe a large debt of gratitude to the many individuals who supplied important research information for this book. Several deserve special mention, and I want to begin with Elsie Elliott Severance. When she was a young girl, Elsie knew Chaplain Scott, and through her letters and personal interviews I came to know Scott as a human being. Many of the personal images of Scott in this book come from Elsie's fond memories, and for her sharing those memories with me, I am profoundly grateful. To Karl Kabelac, assistant librarian for rare books, manuscripts, and archives at the University of Rochester, I owe a special debt for the time he spent not only locating material on Scott in the university's archives but also in doing primary research for me in the records of the Delphic Literary Society. In that same vein I want to thank Evelyn Kirmse, assistant to the president of the University of Arizona, for her research on Scott's service on the university's board of regents and Henrene George, records management supervisor for the American Baptist Churches at Valley Forge, Pennsylvania, for her thorough search of the minute books of the American Baptist Home Missionary Society. I also want to thank Geoffrey P. Mawn, doctoral candidate in history at Arizona State University, who, in the course of his own research on Phoenix, supplied me with scores of newspaper citations on Scott and Scottsdale. To Maurice L. Patterson of the Interlaken Historical Society, Eleanor R. Clise of the Geneva Historical Society, Richard N. Wright of the Onandaga Historical Association, and Doris Cooley of the First Baptist Church of Leavenworth go my sincerest thanks for patiently answering my many letters with pertinent information, old photographs, and valuable new leads. To Californians Yvonne Green of Daly City, DeForeest B. Wright of Hollywood, Bula Mae Saunders of Ukiah, and Lena Polglase of Santa Cruz go my special thanks for sending along a wealth of genealogical and historical information on the Scott family. To Patricia Boettcher who graciously consented to let me use the information she gathered from the files of the *Arizona Republican* and to Mark Feldstein, who spent a summer as my research assistant, I offer my sincere appreciation for their thorough and valuable work. In addition, Bert M. Fireman, Susie Sato, and the staff of the Arizona Historical Foundation deserve special recognition for three years of cheerful, incalculable service to this project. They went out of their way to help me find the information I needed. When it comes to research assistance, however, no one deserves more credit than Fran Carlson. She has been, and continues to be, my indispensable assistant, and I cannot thank her sufficiently for her painstaking research which has added immeasurably to the Arizona chapters of this book.

Several individuals have helped me in ways other than providing information or monetary support, and in closing I want to recognize their efforts. Jonathan Marshall, publisher of the *Scottsdale Daily Progress*, supported this project in many ways, including the generous use of the photographic department of his newspaper to produce negatives from scores of old Scottsdale photographs. His greatest contribution, however, came when he published the first two chapters of this book as a special insert to the *Progress*. That Bicentennial publication not only generated a substantial pre-sale of the Scott biography, but it also helped create a new, sustained awareness of Scottsdale's founder. Albert Camasto, art director for the bureau of publications at Arizona State University, spent untold hours on weekends and at night designing every aspect of this book, and its pleasing, professional look is due to his expertise. William W. Phillips has been my mentor on this project since the day I was hired. Through his patient advising, editing, teaching, and encouraging, he helped make me a better historian, and for that expert guidance I will be forever grateful. And then there is my wife Stevie who did everything for me but write the book. At times she did that, too, when an awkward sentence, a confused idea, or a jumbled paragraph needed revision, and my brain refused to work. From the beginning she typed the letters, the outlines, the notes, and the drafts of the manuscript. She edited, asked questions, and offered ideas. She told me when it was good and when it was bad, and throughout it all she kept me going. To her more than anyone else goes the credit for seeing this project to completion.

The virtues of this book belong to my many associates, but its faults are mine alone.

CHAPTER I

The Young Man
from Farmer Village

Winfield Scott accomplished more in his lifetime than most men could hope to achieve in several lifetimes. There were moments of triumph and moments of defeat, but the thread which ran throughout his life and gave it continuity and substance was service. Winfield Scott spent his life in service: in service to God, in service to his country, in service to his fellowman. He served God throughout his adult life as a Baptist preacher and missionary. He served his country as a line officer in the Civil War and for ten years as a chaplain in the United States Army. He served his fellowman wherever he went and in whatever he did.

In all that he did, he was following and enhancing Scott family traditions. Long before Winfield Scott was born, the members of the Scott family, in their day-to-day lives, had established patterns of behavior and standards of conduct, which, over several generations, became traditions. When he came into this world, Winfield Scott had a vast storehouse of family customs and beliefs from which to draw.

In 1704 David Scott, Winfield's grandfather four generations removed, left Ireland for the New World and began the Scott family tradition of following new paths. He was one of the original proprietors of Ridgefield, Connecticut, and as one of his few recorded acts, he served on the committee charged with buying additional land for the town from the local Indians.[1] Three generations later during the Revolutionary War, Gideon Scott, Winfield's great-grandfather, took up arms against the British. With three brothers, David, James, and Thomas, he fought for the cause of independence and helped establish the Scott tradition of service to country. In 1801 Gideon moved to

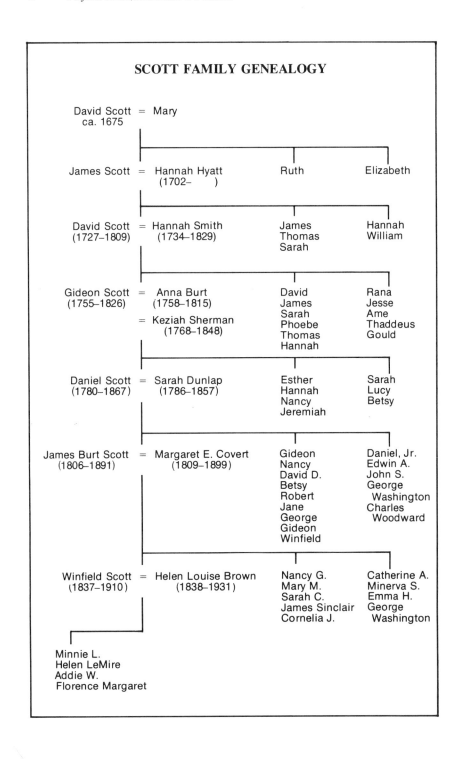

SCOTT FAMILY GENEALOGY

David Scott = Mary
ca. 1675

James Scott = Hannah Hyatt   Ruth   Elizabeth
              (1702–   )

David Scott = Hannah Smith   James   Hannah
(1727–1809)   (1734–1829)   Thomas   William
                                    Sarah

Gideon Scott = Anna Burt   David   Rana
(1755–1826)   (1758–1815)   James   Jesse
                                    Sarah   Ame
             = Keziah Sherman   Phoebe   Thaddeus
               (1768–1848)   Thomas   Gould
                                    Hannah

Daniel Scott = Sarah Dunlap   Esther   Sarah
(1780–1867)   (1786–1857)   Hannah   Lucy
                                    Nancy   Betsy
                                    Jeremiah

James Burt Scott = Margaret E. Covert   Gideon   Daniel, Jr.
(1806–1891)   (1809–1899)   Nancy   Edwin A.
                                         David D.   John S.
                                         Betsy   George
                                         Robert   Washington
                                         Jane   Charles
                                         George   Woodward
                                         Gideon
                                         Winfield

Winfield Scott = Helen Louise Brown   Nancy G.   Catherine A.
(1837–1910)   (1838–1931)   Mary M.   Minerva S.
                                         Sarah C.   Emma H.
                                         James Sinclair George
                                         Cornelia J.   Washington

Minnie L.
Helen LeMire
Addie W.
Florence Margaret

Seneca County, New York, where he put down roots near the shore of Cayuga Lake. Some of his children settled around him, and the nearby crossroads became known as Scotts Corners. One of his sons who settled nearby was Daniel Scott, Winfield's grandfather. He followed in his father's footsteps by serving his country as a captain in the War of 1812. As a Whig he represented Seneca County in the state legislature at Albany and much later would assist in forming the Republican party in New York.[2]

The next Scott to strike out for new lands was Daniel's eldest son James. In 1833 James Burt Scott purchased 160 acres in Oakland County, Michigan, and joined the growing migration to those thinly populated lands northwest of Detroit. Before he left Michigan to return to New York in the mid-1840s, he profitably bought and sold more than 500 acres. In the spring of 1850 a younger brother of James, George Washington Scott, set out for California with seven companions. Stopping in the goldfields to mine for a short time, he arrived in the Sacramento Valley in December 1850 to begin a life of farming and stock raising. In later years George Scott entered the political arena, serving for many years as chairman of the Republican central committee of Yolo County. Twice he ran unsuccessfully for the state legislature, and for a term he held a seat on the Yolo County Board of Supervisors.[3] Winfield, another Scott brother who migrated to Michigan but stayed, served as a member of the Wayne County Board of Supervisors and represented Wayne County in the Michigan legislature. He also served his community as a Baptist preacher.

The Baptist church was a strong influence in the lives of the Scotts. They helped organize congregations, and they served on church boards. They supported their church in both lay capacities and as ministers. In 1827 Keziah Scott, Gideon's second wife, convened the first meeting of the Seneca Baptist Association. This organization was a grouping of Baptist churches from the small towns of the central Finger Lakes region of western New York state and was convened to bring strength and fellowship to its members. In later years Keziah donated the land on which was built the present Ovid Center Baptist Church.[4] Her example is but one of many instances in the Scott family of support for the church.

As the Scotts helped open the country and as they sought to build and defend it, the patterns of their lives helped guide the footsteps of each succeeding generation. In his lifetime of service, Winfield Scott drew from a deep well of inner conviction. That conviction was undoubtedly derived from many sources, not the least of which was a rich family heritage.

Winfield Scott was born February 26, 1837, in the small town of

West Novi, Oakland County, Michigan. He was the first son of James B. and Margaret E. (nee Covert) Scott and the fourth child in a family of three brothers and seven sisters. His boyhood home was a log cabin with windows without glass, and his memories from those early days were of marking trails in the forest, carding and spinning flax and wool, and watching the stagecoach pass along the nearby Detroit and Howell plank-road. Scott spent those early Michigan years in the company of three older sisters, Nancy, Mary, and Sarah. A brother, James Sinclair, was born when Winfield was three, and before the Scotts left Michigan, James and Winfield had two more sisters, Cornelia and Catherine. Little else is known of those early years, and when Winfield was eight or nine, the Scotts returned to western New York state.*

James Scott was a farmer, and Seneca County, where he had grown up and married, was good farm country. He purchased an 181-acre farm in Seneca County near Farmer Village, a small settlement just five miles south of Scotts Corners. Here Winfield grew up as a farm boy. Farms in those days required a great deal of manual labor, and, as the first son, Winfield did his share of tending the livestock, plowing and harrowing, and planting and harvesting the crops. The Scotts lived in the midst of wheat country, and it is probable that James Scott grew wheat as his cash crop. Oats, barley, potatoes, corn, and apples were also grown in this area, but these crops were usually for farm consumption and not for market. Seneca County enjoyed a temperate climate away from the harsh winds of the Great Lakes, and abundant rainfall watered its deep, rich soil.

There were many chores to be done on a Seneca County farm. Women's work included carrying water, making soap, churning butter, cleaning house, cooking, and washing. This burden was shared by Margaret Scott and her three older daughters. The heavier farm work had to be done by Winfield and his father, and James helped with the easier chores. This situation was not as laborious as it might seem, however, because this was "Scott-Covert territory." There were many cousins, brothers, and in-laws in the vicinity to lend a hand when needed. In addition, it was quite common in those days for all the neighbors to work together at harvest time. Each farm in the area was harvested in succession until the work was completed.[5] Winfield's life as a farm boy served him well in later years, and almost everywhere he went, he stayed close to the soil and drew sustenance from it. As much as heritage and service, the land was an important part of Scott's life.

In February 1853, when he was sixteen, young Winfield became a

---

*After returning to New York, the Scotts had three more children; two girls, Minerva and Emma, and one boy, George Washington.

Farmer Village Baptist Church ca. 1860. (Interlaken Historical Society)

Farmer Village School. Winfield Scott received most of his primary education here, less than a half mile from the Scott farm. (Interlaken Historical Society)

member of the Baptist church.[6] At about the same time, he began his preparation for college. With an endless procession of jobs to be done, it is remarkable that James Scott sent his eldest son away to school. He first attended a school in Elbridge, New York, twelve miles west of Syracuse. There were two preparatory schools in Elbridge at that time. Scott probably attended Munro Academy, because this school specialized in the teaching of Latin and Greek, and Scott later took his bachelor of arts degree in the classics. In his senior year he attended Middlebury Academy in Wyoming, New York, twenty-three miles southwest of Rochester. Middlebury was a fine school, and as a Middlebury alumnus Scott found himself in distinguished company. With a maximum enrollment of two hundred, Middlebury through the years graduated seven college presidents, four congressmen, and several judges, state legislators, and professors. Scott's own illustrious record added much to the prestige of Middlebury Academy.

In the fall of 1855, at age eighteen, Scott entered the University of Rochester. As a member of the university's fifth freshman class, he assumed the role of college student with great zest. He found lodging at 24 Monroe Street, enrolled in the freshman classics program, and immediately became involved in university activities.

There were two literary societies on the campus, the Delphic and the Pithonian, and almost every student belonged to one or the other. When, along with twelve of his freshman classmates, he was initiated into the Delphic Literary Society, the event held more than just the usual personal, and transitory, significance. Both literary societies sought to foster among their members the development of writing skills and public speaking abilities. Because their joint debates and individual programs were open to the public and were well attended by the citizens of Rochester, active participation in these academic forums afforded the students more than the customary experience in public speaking. Winfield Scott's speaking and writing skills and the attendant ability to influence and inspire were to have an important impact on the lives of a great many people in the years to come. The development of those skills took place here.

The records of the Delphic Literary Society indicate that Scott was an active member. He participated in debates, critiqued essays, and presented orations. He also served as vice-president, treasurer, and member of the finance committee. Each literary society edited its own paper, and, quite naturally, the Delphic Society's paper was called the *Delphic Oracle*. These papers were more akin to our modern literary journals than to our newspapers, and during his sophomore year, Scott tried his hand at literary editing.

Winfield Scott showed his independent and egalitarian spirit at

Rochester by joining the antisecret fraternity in preference to any of the four secret fraternities. The Greek letters for Scott's fraternity were Delta Upsilon, but the group was known as the "Equitable Fraternity." Clubs and extracurricular activities, of necessity, were secondary to young Scott's course of study. His choice of the classics curriculum meant a rigorous course of instruction. His freshman classes included four in Latin and five in Greek, algebra and geometry, modern history, and English grammar and composition. These classes were divided into three terms, which began in early September and ended with final examinations in early July.

Scott's sophomore year found him residing at 18 New York Street along with classmates Allen Edward Kitchen and David Hamilton Robinson. Kitchen and Robinson were also members of the Delphic Literary Society, and Robinson was a member of Delta Upsilon. Robinson and Scott continued as roommates during their junior and senior years, with Kitchen living next door during their senior year. Like the Three Musketeers, Kitchen, Robinson, and Scott went through their Rochester years together. Kitchen went on to become a minister and did missionary work in the eastern United States and Canada, while Robinson took a doctorate and became a professor of Latin language and literature at the University of Kansas. Good companionship helped bolster their spirits under the weight of an increasingly demanding classics curriculum. The sophomore curriculum included several courses in geometry and trigonometry, Latin, Greek, and French. Rhetoric, physical science, the history of modern literature, and surveying and navigation rounded out the year's course work. To unwind from the rigors of academic life, Scott was a member of a chess club and, in the spring, played baseball.

At the beginning of his junior year, Scott moved to 15 University Hall. At that time University Hall housed the entire campus of the university, in addition to the Rochester Theological Seminary. Situated in a busy commercial district, the building was an old hotel that had been converted to university use. It was located on Buffalo Street near the towpath for the Erie Canal and had been built originally to attract canal passengers who wished a respite from their journey. The windows, which opened on the front of the four-story building, gave a clear view of the boats plying the canal as well as of the bustling horse traffic on the street below. The hotel's dining room became the university's chapel and was used for both morning prayers and large lectures. The cellar became a dining hall run by the janitor and his family. Additional cellar space provided washrooms for the sixty-five or more students who lived on the upper floors of the main building and in a three-story west wing. University Hall also contained a library, classrooms, study

The Finger Lakes Region of Western New York State

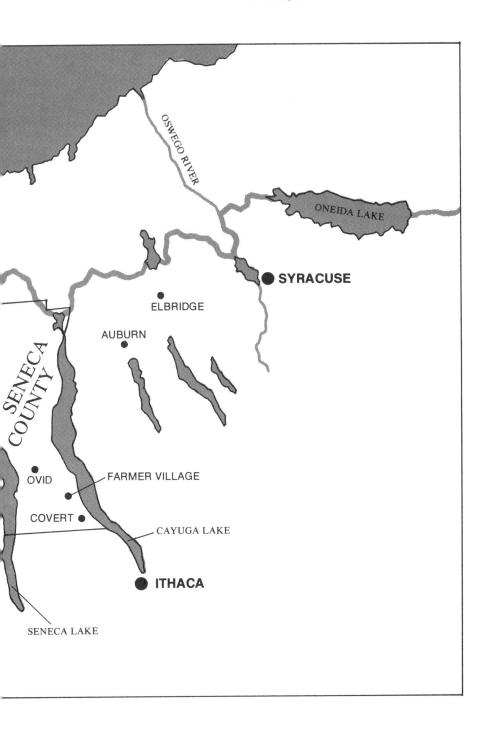

halls, and permanent meeting rooms for the literary societies and university trustees.[7] Here Scott was to spend the next four years of his life, first as an upperclassman at Rochester and then as a student at Rochester Theological Seminary.

Seven courses in the physical sciences dominated the junior curriculum; German replaced French; two courses in Greek and one in Latin were added; and a second course in rhetoric and one in logic completed the third-year course of study. In addition to his work with the Delphic Literary Society, the young man from Farmer Village took time to be· an editor of the first *Interpres Universitatis*. This publication was the precursor of the modern yearbook, listing the membership rosters of the various organizations and the winners of the class prizes. It also presented a lighthearted recounting of the past year. Writing humorously of the university's genesis in humble surroundings, the editors of this first yearbook created a graphic image of the neighborhood of the University of Rochester. "Instantly a beautiful temple sprung up on the shore of the loud sounding canal . . . amid groceries [and] cabbage shops."

Amid groceries and cabbage shops Scott began his senior year at Rochester and found himself engaged in a mind-expanding course of study. Philosophy, law, religion, history, economics, Plato, and Cicero were but seven of the twelve senior courses required to complete the baccalaureate degree in the classics. On July 13, 1859, Winfield Scott graduated from the University of Rochester. He had done the myriad things a college student does, but, more important, he had accomplished something unique in his family. He had gone to college. The young boy from the small farm community was becoming the young man about to make his way in the world, a way that would touch the lives of thousands of people. The University of Rochester was his springboard, and his having been there can be attributed to the work and sacrifice of his father, a sacrifice not uncommon in American history.

Not seeming to break stride, Scott entered Rochester Theological Seminary (now Colgate-Rochester) and began his preparation for the ministry. In taking up the ministry, he was following the family tradition of service to the Baptist church. This young seminarian must have taken some time from his studies, however, for two years later, on the day of his graduation, he married Helen Louise Brown. Helen Brown was born January 8, 1838, in Plainfield, New York. She grew up and went to school there, and took teacher training at nearby Richfield Seminary. Her first teaching job was in Ogden, New York, ten miles west of Rochester, and it was there that she met Winfield Scott. The couple was married in Ogden and soon journeyed to Farmer Village

Margaret E. and James B. Scott and their seven daughters ca. 1860s. The only daughter identified is Nancy Scott Boorom on the extreme right. (Interlaken Historical Society)

Helen Louise Scott ca. 1862. (Interlaken Historical Society)

where the Seneca Baptist Association licensed the new preacher in the church where he had been baptized some eight years before.[8] The Reverend Mr. Scott and his bride had little time to themselves, for in late July they moved to Syracuse where Scott succeeded the Reverend John T. Seeley who was leaving his post as pastor of the Second Baptist Church. With the cloud of civil war hanging over the country, it was an unsettling time to begin a ministerial career.

Scott took charge of his flock just as the Union's thoughts of a quick and easy war were being dispelled at the Battle of Bull Run. He set about the task of winning the confidence of his congregation and the saving of their souls, and being a zealous young clergyman, he quickly won the respect and affection not only of his own congregation but of the community as well. The young pastor's ordination service took place December 13, 1861, with Dr. E. G. Robinson, president of Rochester Theological Seminary, journeying to Syracuse to preach the sermon. As the holiday season approached, the nation's flag was prominently displayed behind the Christmas tree at the Second Baptist Church. The people's thoughts were divided between the joy of Christmas and the sorrow of civil war. As the guns of war grew louder, Scott was torn between service to God and service to country, but he stayed with his congregation during the first year of fighting.

In July 1862 President Lincoln issued a call for three hundred thousand volunteers. This call, received with scant enthusiasm in many quarters, prompted Scott to action. He believed fervently in the preservation of the Union, and after receiving a temporary leave of absence from his church, he began to tour the countryside urging young men to answer the call. At one of these meetings a young man shouted out, "Oh, it's all right for you to talk. If you'll organize a company, I'll go." The challenge affected Scott deeply and hastened his decision. Soon thereafter he addressed a special meeting of his church and asked to be granted an indefinite leave of absence. He explained his inner turmoil, the growing, compelling feeling that he must answer his country's call with a personal commitment. It had become clear to him that his commitment must be to raise a company of men and to lead them into battle. "He had become convinced that it was his duty to lay down the pen for awhile and take up the sword." With deep regret, the congregation released its pastor from his duties and bade him "God's speed" in his perilous endeavors.

CHAPTER II

The Fighting Parson

It was becoming increasingly difficult to induce young men to enlist, and President Lincoln's call for volunteers elicited little response. The ardor of potential recruits paled before the realities of war, while plentiful jobs and high wages solidified their interest at home. Nevertheless, the troops had to be raised, and on August 4, 1861, the administration changed its approach by calling on the states to enlist three hundred thousand men in the militia. The president could not conscript men into federal service, but he could draft the state militia. Not wanting to be saddled with the political liability of drafting constituents into the militia, state and local officials vigorously encouraged volunteer regiments and offered attractive bounties to fill their quotas.[1] In this milieu, Winfield Scott quickly gained permission to hold meetings and raise troops.

Returning to his boyhood home of Farmer Village, the young minister quickly recruited a company of ninety-eight men from the surrounding towns and farms. Thirty cousins joined Scott, and many men came from his former Sunday school class. He also took the entire town band, twelve members strong,* and a local glee club. The majority of his recruits were farmers, but there were masons, tailors, carpenters, and blacksmiths as well. Several merchants, an engineer, a photographer, and a printer also enlisted in the Union's cause under Scott.[2] His first lieutenant, Thomas R. Lounsbury, had graduated from

---

*The Farmer Village band became one of the "most distinguished bands in the Union Army." Selected as the brigade band, it later played at the Washington's Birthday ball described in the opening pages of Bruce Catton's *A Stillness at Appomattox* and gave the signal for the four hundred-gun salute when General Robert E. Lee surrendered.

Yale at the same time Scott had graduated from Rochester. In New York writing for Appleton's *New American Encyclopedia* when the call came for volunteers, Lounsbury returned to his home town of Ovid, just down the road from Farmer Village, in time to enlist in Scott's company. Lounsbury would go on to an illustrious career as a scholar. He was a professor of English at Yale from 1871 to 1906, one of the fifteen original members of the American Academy of Arts and Letters, and in 1896 he became a fellow in the American Academy of Arts and Sciences. His three volumes, *Studies in Chaucer*, "remain one of the great classics of Chaucerian scholarship."[3] But now he was a twenty-four-year-old first lieutenant who, along with some one hundred other young men of his company, knew nothing of soldiering but who would have to learn quickly.

When Scott and his men reported to regimental headquarters at Geneva, they were organized as Company C, 126th Regiment, New York Volunteer Infantry. The date was August 9, 1862.[4] The Reverend Mr. Scott became Captain Scott. Four days later the members of the Second Baptist Church of Syracuse went for an outing in the country. Filling seven cars of an excursion train, they took a thirty-mile ride to the foot of Cayuga Lake. There in a wooded glen the cares and worries of a country at war were forgotten for a while. Song and laughter filled the air as children played on swings set up for the occasion, and adults rowed and sailed on the lake. Midway through the festivities, Captain Scott arrived from Geneva and received a sword, belt, and sash from the members of his congregation.* In replying to this gesture of affection and respect, the young captain bade farewell to his friends of one year. Tears came to the eyes of many. The reality of war had reached them in a personal way.

The 126th Regiment was mustered into service on August 22, and left the state four days later. It was assigned to the Middle Department, Eighth Army Corps and sent to Harper's Ferry, Virginia.[5] Colonel Dixon S. Miles, commander of the Union garrison at Harper's Ferry, first assigned the 126th to active duty on September 5, just as the Confederate Army of Northern Virginia crossed the Potomac into Maryland. The Army of the Potomac under General John Pope had been defeated at the Second Battle of Bull Run and was retreating toward the defenses of Washington. Robert E. Lee wanted to keep moving, to harass the enemy, and to take the war from Virginia's ravaged soil. His ultimate goal was to bring the Federals out from the defenses of Washington and into a decisive battle, which he believed he

---

*In later years Scott would remark that it was a beautiful sword, inscribed with the date and the name of the church. He also made the comment that "As one looks back upon it now, it seems a queer thing that a church should supply weapons, but it shows the spirit of the times."

Captain Winfield Scott ca. 1862. (Interlaken Historical Society)

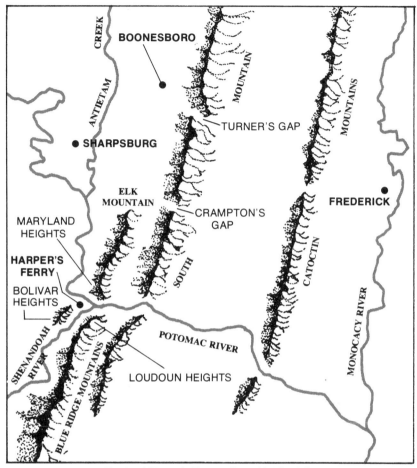

Battle of Harper's Ferry   Sept. 12–15, 1862

could win. He thought that a harassing movement into Maryland might bring the Yankees out for a fight. Arriving at Frederick, Maryland, Lee decided to move behind the screen of South Mountain. He knew that the Union command would be nervous not knowing what his army was about. They would have to come out to find him and to protect Union soil.[6]

A threat to Lee's maneuver was the large Union garrison at Harper's Ferry. The garrison was to the rear of Lee's forces and across his lines of communication. It had to be removed. Stonewall Jackson, with several divisions, moved to capture the garrison while Lee crossed South Mountain toward Hagerstown.

The men of the 126th New York were as green as recruits could be. Unarmed until they reached Harper's Ferry, undrilled in military maneuvers, they were not instructed in the loading and firing of their weapons until the advance patrols of Jackson's forces made contact with Union pickets. The officers of the 126th were also inexperienced in military procedures. Most of them had never commanded men in battle. Their colonel, however, stood ready for a fight, and when the call came to reinforce the Union brigade on Maryland Heights, Colonel Eliakim Sherill volunteered his regiment.

Maryland Heights was the key to the defense of Harper's Ferry. So long as the Federals held the Heights, the Confederates could not take Harper's Ferry. Consisting of the southern extremities of Elk Mountain, the Heights overlooked the Potomac River and the town, and from that vantage point, the other defenses of Harper's Ferry, the approaches to the town, and the town itself could be murderously pounded by artillery. Here the battle for possession of Harper's Ferry, its garrison, and its mountain of supplies would be won or lost.

When word came on Friday, September 12, that the Confederates were attacking in force, Colonel Miles called for reinforcements, and the 126th marched for the Heights. They arrived about one hour before sunset and formed a battle line on the crest of the mountain. There was some sharp skirmishing until dark when the lines quieted down. The men of the 126th slept on their muskets that night without food or water and within earshot of the Confederate lines. At daybreak the Confederates took up their skirmishing with a company of the 126th and a company of the Thirty-second Ohio. The Rebels began pushing the Yankees back, but the Federals soon rallied and drove back the enemy. The Federal line let out a shout at this turn of events and unwittingly revealed its position and strength. Half an hour later General Joseph B. Kershaw's South Carolina brigade, numbering approximately nine hundred men, attacked in force, pushed back the Yankee skirmishers again, and brought their fire to bear on the main Federal line. In addition to the 126th New York, there were three companies of the Third Maryland Regiment and possibly three companies of the Thirty-second Ohio Regiment. In all, approximately twelve hundred Yankees held the line until heavy fire forced them to give ground. Some men ran, but most retreated as best they could through a tangle of trees, thick entangling underbrush, and large rocks to a breastworks a quarter-mile to the rear. There Colonel Sherill rallied his forces and stopped the Rebel advance.

Some of General Kershaw's South Carolinians then tried to flank the Union line on the left. This position was held by Captain Scott's company, and the captain turned his men to face the enemy. When the troops from South Carolina were about thirty yards away, Scott ordered his men to fire and then countercharge. The Confederates had had to attack uphill on a thirty-degree grade. The countercharge downhill, at that angle, was irresistible. Although Scott and his men were outnumbered three to one, they swept the Confederates off the hill. Leading the charge, Scott was wounded in the right leg. A one-ounce musket ball imbedded itself in the bone below his right knee but did not break the leg. After he replaced his men in line, Scott reported his encounter to Colonel Sherill, who noticed his wound and ordered him to the rear. Scott refused and remained to fight until loss of blood brought him to the brink of unconsciousness. He was again ordered from the field, and this time he complied. Although painfully wounded, Scott was lucky. His pants carried five other bullet holes.

While Kershaw's men attacked the center and left of the Union line, General William Barksdale maneuvered his Mississippi brigade, over nine hundred strong, down the side of the mountain around the Union right. They slipped in behind the Union forces undetected, and when they opened fire, the startled Yankees panicked. Caught in a crossfire and holding the breastworks virtually alone, the confused New Yorkers broke and ran. Colonel Sherill valiantly tried to rally his men, but he was soon wounded in the face and carried from the field. Without seasoned veterans or even men like Sherill and Scott to calm and control the 126th, the panic quickly spread, and there was no stopping the rout.

Attempts were made to retake the breastworks, but they failed, and late in the afternoon the Union forces abandoned the Heights to the Confederates. Jackson's forces on the Heights spent the next day moving up artillery while his other divisions attempted to take Bolivar Heights and Loudoun Heights to complete the circle. The bombardment of Harper's Ferry during September 14 and 15 was devastating. The shelling could be heard in Centreville, Virginia, some thirty miles distant. The Federals returned the fire until they exhausted their ammunition. At 8:00 A.M. on the fifteenth, the Union garrison, 11,200 men, surrendered. Since the Confederate forces were needed at Sharpsburg, along Antietam Creek, the Union prisoners, Captain Scott among them, were almost immediately paroled. They swore not to take up arms until properly exchanged for Confederate prisoners and set out upon the road to Frederick, Maryland. Captain Scott lay sick at Frederick for several days, unable to move. When he could travel, he went home to Farmer Village to have the musket ball removed from the bone of his right leg. His regiment was sent to Chicago for guard duty at Camp Douglas.

A military tribunal was convened in late September to investigate what many Union officers considered the shameful abandonment of

Maryland Heights and the unnecessary surrender of Harper's Ferry. During the extensive examination of witnesses, the acting adjutant of the 126th New York, Lieutenant Samuel Barras, was called upon to testify. Lieutenant Barras was asked what officers he had seen try to rally the 126th when it broke and ran. He replied that he had seen Colonel Sherill, the commander of the 126th. Barras was asked if he had seen any other officers. He answered that he had seen Captain Phillips try to rally his men before Colonel Sherill was wounded. "Do you recollect any other officer besides Captain Phillips?" asked the court. "Yes, sir. There was Captain Scott, a very brave man who stood through the whole thing until he was wounded." That statement epitomizes Captain Scott's entire Civil War experience. Scott's regiment was censured for its behavior on Maryland Heights, but it seems clear from reading the testimony that many of the charges filed against the 126th came from officers trying to camouflage their own guilt. All circumstances considered, the men of the 126th held up as well as could be expected of raw recruits. There would be other battles which would vindicate their honor. They became a much bloodied and much decorated unit,* and leading them through some of their fiercest fighting was the captain of Company C. Like his grandfather and great-grandfather, he fought for the country he loved and risked his life for what he believed.

Captain Scott's general health was greatly impaired by his ordeal. The doctors had had to enlarge the wound in the head of the tibia to extract the lead ball, and the surgical lesion was slow to close and mend. He remained at home in Farmer Village with his wife and parents, while his regiment spent two months guarding Confederate prisoners at Camp Douglas. Declared exchanged November 22, 1862, the regiment moved back to Washington, D.C., where it went into camp at Arlington Heights, Virginia, just across the Potomac from the Capital. On the afternoon of December 3, the 126th boarded a train for Union Mills, Virginia, and the outer defenses of Washington. Union Mills was a station on the Orange and Alexandria Railway where it crossed Bull Run. It was about twenty miles southwest of Washington and represented the outer extremity of Union sovereignty in Virginia.

On January 1, 1863, the impatient captain reported to Secretary of War Edwin M. Stanton in Washington. Although still on crutches, he strenuously pleaded with Stanton to be returned to active duty and was allowed to join his regiment on January 3, as it patrolled the lower reaches of Bull Run. Here was beautiful country. Rolling meadowland,

---

*In terms of losses, killed and wounded, as a percentage of total strength, the 126th New York stood eleventh among the four hundred fighting regiments of the war.

gently rising hills, majestic ramparts, and towering pines combined to camouflage the blood that had been spilled here. But here also was a country scarred by war. Once thriving farms had fallen into decay. Fields went unplowed. Forests were scorched by fire. The people were gone. Bull Run had lent its name twice to battles, and only those few people who were "bound to it by an iron necessity" stayed on the land. "While ground is getting to be historic, it loses altogether its attraction as a residence for human beings."[7]

It was a cold, gray winter. Frequent storms, both snow and rain, pelted the soldiers as they stared out across Bull Run, searching for phantom "Johnny Rebs" among the pines. The snow and rain turned the Virginia soil into a quagmire and made patrolling the long perimeter a miserable experience. Officers and men went on duty every other day, slogging their way through their own personal "slough of despond." For Captain Scott, on crutches, it must have been doubly difficult. For two months, while marching his men the two miles to the picket line, he never fell behind because of his wound. As captain of the picket, Scott patrolled the line night and day, always on crutches, and never missed a turn.

On March 1 a competitive drill was held among the companies of General John J. Abercrombie's division. Captain Scott and his company won the competition. The company was honored by being made division provost guard, and Captain Scott was made assistant provost marshal. It proved to be a depressing assignment. The provost marshal, in exercising his traditional policeman's role, dealt with the local residents. He issued passes for them to go about their business and handled local disputes. These people held Southern sympathies, only barely masked, and viewed with contempt the Union forces occupying their neighborhood. The young women, in particular, did not bother to conceal their feelings and freely insulted the Union soldiers. With eyes dulled by sorrow and hopelessness, these border people, caught between two worlds, aimlessly grubbed out an existence. It must have especially saddened the young clergyman turned captain to witness this tableau day after day.

Toward the end of March, headquarters were transferred from Union Mills to Centreville, and with it went the brigade to which the 126th New York was attached. In early April the heaviest snowstorm of the winter blanketed the countryside and punctuated the end to a bitter season. With the spring came the wives and some of the daughters of many of the Union officers. The presence of female society was an elixir to the men, and picnics with music and dancing buoyed their spirits. There were protestations from division headquarters that these wives and daughters were in the way and should return to Washington, but they stood their ground and graced the dress parades of the various regiments. All was quiet along the outer defenses of Washington, and the only thing to spoil the spring idyll was six hours of daily drill.

During the winter just past, the Lincoln administration had decided to form Negro combat regiments, and on April 6 Captain Scott volunteered to command one. He thought he could be of greater service to the Union in that capacity, but what happened to the application is not known. Scott remained with the 126th. It is known, however, that he received strong recommendations in support of the application from his regimental commander, Colonel Sherill, and from his brigade commander, General Alexander Hays. Said Colonel Sherill of Captain Scott, "He was wounded in the engagement on Maryland Heights while manfully performing his duty and on that occasion displayed the truest courage." Added General Hays, "If the Department has demand for the services specified, of an officer, I know no one more worthy, or better qualified than Captain Scott." Winfield Scott received little official recognition of his exemplary service during the Civil War. In that disappointment, he must have cherished the great respect in which he was held by his brother officers.

With General Joseph Hooker's retreat from Chancellorsville came exceedingly warm weather, and the spring slipped slowly toward summer. The officer of the day sat in his tent drinking lemonade and writing letters. The officer of the outposts lay in the grass and watched the breeze play with the stately pines. There was no inkling of what the summer would bring. The war might just as well have been on another continent.

Then suddenly rumors became reality, and the idyll was over. On the fifteenth of June riders came galloping up to division headquarters, and the news spread like wildfire. The Army of the Potomac was on its way. Late in the day huge clouds of dust that almost obliterated the southern sky made believers of the skeptics. They were coming to find Lee. General Robert E. Lee had been on the march for almost two weeks, moving up the Shenandoah Valley through Maryland and into Pennsylvania. As Lee moved into Pennsylvania, the Union forces were presented with an opportunity to catch this formidable enemy in alien territory. If he were vulnerable anywhere, it would be on northern soil.[8]

As corps after corps passed through Centreville, Scott and his comrades wondered if they would be left behind. The answer came on June 23. Their brigade had been transferred to General Winfield Scott Hancock's Second Corps and told to stand by with ten days' rations. As a part of the Army of the Potomac, they marched off to Gettysburg with an exhilaration not felt for many months. About a month later their brigade would pass this way again, going south in pursuit of Lee. In the hellish interim they would have left behind in graves and hospitals two-thirds of their comrades.[9]

Captain Scott's wound still had not healed, and he was quite lame. In late April he had spent some time in the U.S. General Hospital in Washington, but the wound showed no improvement. The surgeons doubted his ability to make the march north and wanted him to report to them for assignment in the rear. Scott refused and reported for duty with his company. He was determined to be in the coming fight if his

Points of Reference for the 126th New York Volunteers

legs would carry him. As the Second Corps started north, Scott and his men were assigned to guard the supply train. If the staff had hoped to detail the captain to easy duty, its plan went awry. The first night out, the train was attacked by Colonel John S. Mosby's raiders. Scott and his men fought the famous Confederate guerillas all night and drove them off without losing a wagon. The strenuous march to Gettysburg continued to irritate Scott's wound. To prevent infection, he kept it open and clean by probing it two or three inches each day. Pieces of bone and a tattered bit of his "long-johns," which had been driven into his leg by the musket ball at Harper's Ferry, worked themselves out along the march. Nevertheless, he walked the entire distance.

While the Army of the Potomac deployed along dusty Pennsylvania roads searching for Lee's Army of Northern Virginia, General George Meade succeeded General Hooker in command. Lee was rumored heading in the direction of Gettysburg, and Hancock's Second Corps made a forced march of thirty-three miles to try and find him. Along the way, the corps forded a stream, but the troops were forbidden to take off their shoes and stockings. The day was hot, and before five miles had been covered, the men of the Second Corps began dropping out along the dusty road with badly blistered feet. By nightfall over 80 percent of the Second Corps was out of action. Only twelve of Captain Scott's effective company of sixty men answered roll call that evening, and his was the highest percentage of duty-ready men in the regiment. The Second Corps was delayed twenty-four hours, its men unable to move on painful feet and, as a result, was not available to reinforce the badly beleaguered Union forces during the first day of battle at Gettysburg. From such seemingly insignificant incidents are the greater events of history often constructed. Henceforward, on hot days the men were required to ford streams barefooted.

On July 1 the opposing armies met at a sleepy crossroads called Gettysburg. Neither Lee nor Meade had chosen that place for battle, but their armies, once engaged, began to fight, and the battle was joined in earnest.[10] Captain Scott recalled that as the Second Corps marched toward Gettysburg, they heard the boom of cannon, announcing that Lee had been found. All that day the Second Corps hurried toward the sound of battle. They finally made camp at 10:00 P.M., only three miles from the battle lines. The next morning the Second Corps was positioned in the Union line near Ziegler's Grove on Cemetery Ridge. The 126th New York was about to experience its first fighting since Harper's Ferry. They were a part of the Third Brigade of the Third Division of Hancock's Second Corps, and in the twilight of early evening, Hancock sent them to reinforce General Daniel E. Sickles on the Union left.

Since 3:00 P.M. the Union line had been under heavy artillery attack. Under that cover, Confederate General James Longstreet had launched an assault on Sickles' overextended forces. The Union troops gave ground grudgingly, but by late afternoon the Confederates were about to cave in Sickles' entire position. Hancock sent his Third Division to fill the gaps in Sickles' line, and the 126th went into action. With the 125th New York on their left and the 111th New York on their right, they faced three Mississippi regiments in a marshy thicket near the source of Plum Run. The Southerners were part of General Barksdale's Mississippi brigade which had pushed the 126th off Maryland Heights. Without additional support, the New Yorkers charged the thicket and drove the Mississippians from their cover. This they accomplished in the face of a murderous fire that hit them only ten paces from the thicket. The Mississippians were routed, many throwing themselves down and surrendering. Scott and his company recaptured the battery of five guns that Barksdale had earlier seized from Sickles' men. As they chased the remaining Rebels toward the Emmitsburg Road, they came under artillery fire from two sides and withdrew. The entire Third Division was under heavy attack and was finally forced to retreat having lost three of four brigade commanders and a third of its men killed or wounded. More Union regiments were sent to reinforce the left, and by dark the line was secured. The Third Division, including the 126th, returned to its original position on Cemetery Ridge.[11]

The next morning four companies of the 126th got into another fight, this time near Ziegler's Grove. Captain Scott and his company were in the midst of this skirmishing, which Scott described as the hottest he had ever experienced. They charged the enemy's line along the Emmitsburg Road and, after a heavy exchange of volleys, drove it back into a wheat field across the road. Hidden in the wheat field, a Rebel brigade that had been held in reserve shot the advancing Yankees to pieces. The captains of the three other companies were killed, and Scott lost over a third of his company. The twelve bullet holes in his hat, coat, and trousers showed that the young captain's luck was holding. At 11:00 A.M. Scott and his men were relieved, and as they passed through their own lines, he noticed that the entire line had grown quiet.

At noon it was "as still as the Sabbath." The July sun bore down on the men as they sat eating lunch from their haversacks. Some wrote letters home, while others discussed the fighting of the past two days. General John Gibbon's mess staff had found and prepared an old rooster, and Generals Meade, Hancock, and Gibbon, along with some staff officers, sat down to a hot meal.[12] "The silence and the heat were oppressive . . ." At one o'clock a signal shot was fired, and 130 Rebel guns shattered the silence. Lee was preparing a final assault, this time against the Union center, and to ease the way, his gunners were laying down a horrifying barrage. They were soon answered by 80 Union cannon, and the heaviest bombardment in North American history had begun. In a one square mile area more than 200 guns were getting off two to three rounds a minute. The noise was so deafening the Union gunners reported later they could barely hear the reports of their own weapons.[13] The estimates vary of how long the bombardment lasted, but Captain Scott reported that it lasted for an hour and a half. He and his men, and the rest of the Second and Third Divisions, lay beneath the crest of Cemetery Ridge and hugged the earth for dear life. Men in the infantry usually wisecracked during a cannonade to help break the tension, but this time they were quiet. No one could make himself heard above the roar of the bombardment, but more important, no one had been through anything like this before, and all were stunned into silence.

In later years, however, Scott recalled with humor his feelings during that shelling. "I was not a heavy weight then," he said, "but I remember my most sincere regret as I lay there flattened out like a postage stamp, was that I was not thinner." The shells that burst among them killed their comrades and threw up so much earth that they were almost buried. Their only salvation that day was the aim of the Confederate gunners. They were firing too high, and they did a great deal more damage to the rear areas than they did to the lines of infantry.[14] Casualties to the 126th New York and to most of the Third Division remained relatively light, and with that realization, the men waited quietly for the firing to end.

The shelling slackened and finally ceased. Scott and his men moved forward to the crest of the ridge. On their left was the 108th New York commanded by Lieutenant Colonel Francis E. Pierce, a classmate of Scott at Rochester. As they walked toward the front, the old classmates locked arms, and Pierce said, "Well, Scott, we . . . sat beside each other in the classroom many a day; but this is a new experience. This isn't much like digging out Greek roots." What they were about to see was indeed a new experience. From the top of the ridge, they overlooked the entire valley. Out of the woods and from behind breastworks on the opposite ridge stepped fifteen thousand Confederate soldiers. In the center of the line General George E. Pickett deployed his five thousand Virginians; Pickett's charge was about to begin. First came a heavy skirmish line, then another, then the first line of battle. Behind them marched the regimental officers, and behind them, mounted and sabers drawn, came the brigade and division commanders. Then came the second line of battle, in the same order as the first, and behind them still, were the massed columns of supports and reserves. The lines stretched for a mile from flank to flank. The guidons and regimental flags were unfurled, and the men carried their muskets at right shoulder with sunlight gleaming from thousands of barrels. The men dressed ranks as if on parade, and then they came like a "river of silver" moving toward the Union lines.

It was a magnificent sight that no man present would ever forget. The lines remained straight and in perfect order. Captain Scott was totally captivated by the majesty before him. "I was so absorbed with the beauty and grandeur of the scene that I became oblivious to the shells that were bursting about us. This passage of scripture came to my mind, and I repeated it aloud: 'Fair as the moon, bright as the sun, and terrible as an army with banners.' "* The Confederate lines did a half wheel left and came straight for the position defended by Hancock's Third Division. Their left flank would strike where Scott and his men were stationed. As the Confederate lines moved forward they were laced again and again with shot and shell. Gaps opened in the lines and were heroically closed again. On they came in perfect order. Kneeling behind a low stone wall, the Yankee battle line waited. As the Confederate lines approached, they brought their guns from the shoulder to the charge position. Moments seemed ages. A few steps farther, and the Confederates raised their weapons and fired. Then they let out a Rebel yell and charged the stone wall. The Yankees stood as one man and fired. The Confederates went down "like grass before the scythe." Scott and the men of the 126th had moved out on the right as the Rebels closed, and now they caught them in a murderous flanking fire. The Confederates soon broke, and the 126th charged their flank and routed them. They captured many prisoners and three stands of enemy colors.[15] All along the line repeated Confederate charges were repulsed. As the Rebels were beaten back, the valley became a sea of frantic, confused men. Confederate officers tried to regroup their forces but failed. The Confederate charge was spent. The Battle of Gettysburg was over.

It had been a costly battle for both sides. The Confederates lost

---

*Confederate General Daniel Harvey Hill recalled that same biblical quotation back in the fall of 1862 as he sat atop South Mountain and watched the Army of the Potomac streaming across the Catoctin Ridge on its way to find Robert E. Lee. Waiting in reserve at Boonsboro while Stonewall Jackson and his command hammered the Union garrison at Harper's Ferry, Hill received word from Confederate patrols that "quite a lot of Yankees" seemed headed in his direction, and he went to reconnoiter the situation with part of his command. [Bruce Catton, *Mr. Lincoln's Army* (Garden City, N. Y.: Doubleday and Co., 1951), pp. 215, 221, 231–35.] Watching the blue battle lines, flags unfurled, marching across the valley between the ridge and his position, Hill viewed a scene similar to the one Winfield Scott observed from the other side at Gettysburg. Even though Scott was a biblical scholar, it is a commentary on the times that both men chose a scriptural passage, and the same one at that, to reflect their feelings as they viewed the ancient pageant spread out before them.

25,000 men, killed or wounded. The Union forces sustained 23,000 casualties.[16] The losses of the 126th New York were the third highest of any regiment at Gettysburg. It lost 231 men including Colonel Eliakim Sherill. Captain Scott was wounded twice at Gettysburg neither time severely. He remained in the field and saw the battle through to the end.

After Gettysburg the Army of the Potomac was tired, and Lee's Army of Northern Virginia retreated across the Potomac back onto home ground. The fall of 1863 saw a series of offensives and counteroffensives with neither side gaining much by its efforts. As the armies went into winter quarters, Captain Winfield Scott was placed on special duty. His previous recruiting success had not gone unnoticed, and in February 1864 he was sent back to his home state. Headquartered at Canandaigua, New York, he toured the Finger Lakes region recruiting men for the Union cause. On special duty for about two months, he rejoined his regiment in early April, as the Army of the Potomac prepared to move out.

On March 9, 1864, Ulysses S. Grant was promoted to lieutenant general and general-in-chief of the armies of the United States. As spring approached, he took personal command of the Army of the Potomac and proposed a campaign against Richmond. Grant's actual goal was the Army of Northern Virginia. If he could engage Lee and never lose contact, by sheer weight of numbers he could decimate the Army of Northern Virginia and end the war. On a sunny May morning, with this strategy in mind, Grant crossed the Rapidan and entered a second-growth stand of timber and underbrush called the Wilderness.[17]

Captain Winfield Scott had been put in command of the 126th New York on May 1, and he now led his regiment into a gloomy, treacherous morass of underbrush, marshy bogs, and stunted trees. There were no roads to speak of, only small country lanes. It was an impossible place for a battle, and that is why Lee chose it. Outnumbered and outgunned, he needed an equalizer. The three nightmarish days in the Wilderness accomplished little. It was a total waste of human resources. The Union forces suffered approximately seventeen thousand casualties and the Confederates about half that number.[18] In the midst of this hellish battle Captain Scott was given command of the 125th New York as well. The Union was running short of officers, and more and more responsibility devolved upon those who survived.[19]

As Grant tried to flank Lee after the Wilderness, their armies collided at another sleepy crossroads, Spotsylvania Court House.[20] North of the courthouse, the Confederates constructed a salient of log breastworks and trenches nearly a mile deep and half a mile wide. On May 12 elements of Hancock's Second Corps attacked the blunt angle

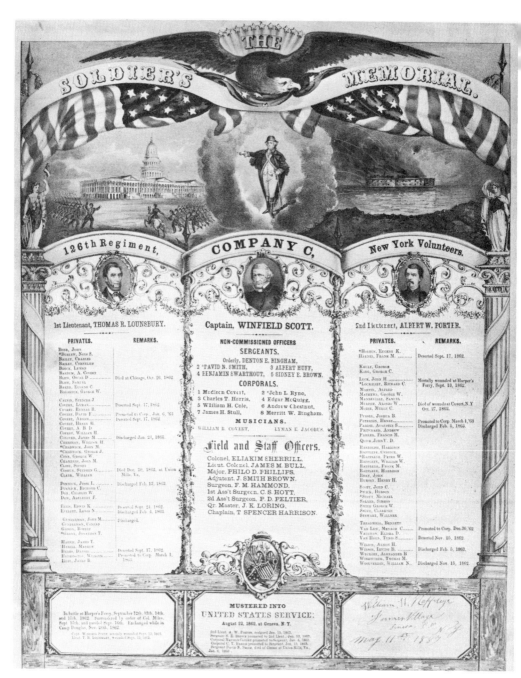

Currier and Ives color print containing the roster of Company C, 126th Regiment, New York Volunteer Infantry. (Interlaken Historical Society)

of the salient and started an insane pitched battle which a member of the Iron Brigade called, "the most terrible twenty-four hours of our service in the war."[21]

While leading a charge that day, Captain Scott was wounded in the chest, but the force of the musket ball was spent on the Bible that he carried in his pocket. He was out of action only for the remainder of that day and resumed command the next morning. Just five days later, he was wounded again. Before going into battle on May 18, Scott asked to see one of his regimental chaplains. From his pocket he took a silver pen, the one he had used throughout college and seminary, the one with which he had written his love letters and sermons. As he gave it to his fellow officer, he said, "Chaplain, I'm going to be hit this morning; I don't know whether I am to be killed or not; If I am, see that my wife gets this pen, and tell her I thought of her, and tell my old mother that I died game."

In a charge against a breastworks that morning, an artillery shell tore off a large portion of the inside of his right thigh. Following the battle, the army doctors went among the wounded deciding who could be saved and who they believed to be mortally wounded. Captain Scott was given up for dead, but he did not see it that way. With what little strength he had left, he raised a musket in the direction of the doctors and demanded to be taken to the field hospital. John Ryno, one of the Farmer Village band members whom Scott had recruited, was on stretcher duty that day and helped carry his captain from the field. Scott saw the chaplain as he was being carried to the rear and called to him. "Here, chaplain, give me that pen—I will take it home myself, now." The doctors, however, were not so sanguine about his future. Winfield Scott's service on the battlefield had come to an end.

Helen Scott was notified of her husband's grave condition and set out to be by his side. She traveled to Washington hoping to obtain a pass to go to the front. She was refused but not easily deterred. While attending a morning reception, she met President Lincoln and won a personal interview with him. Being a persuasive woman and having a worthwhile cause, Helen Scott obtained her needed pass from the president. By this time Captain Scott had been moved to Union Mills, and she hurried there to care for him. Army field hospitals during the Civil War were notorious for their sorely inadequate care. Wounds were often bandaged in soiled rags, and wounded limbs were usually amputated. Care often consisted only of changing the hay upon which the wounded men slept. Helen Scott quickly made arrangements to take her husband home, and there, amid the warmth of his family, Captain Scott slowly regained his health.

Winfield Scott's gallantry in action had impressed his superiors as he commanded two regiments through the Battles of the Wilderness and Spotsylvania Court House. Both Scott's division commander, General Francis C. Barlow, and his brigade commander, Colonel Clinton D. MacDougall, recommended him for promotion to the colonelcy of his regiment. But this honor was not to be his. Although the war committee of his military district unanimously supported his commission, it was denied him by New York Governor Horatio Seymour. Seymour was a Democrat who vociferously opposed the war.[22] He was up for reelection in the fall of 1864, and granting a colonel's commission to a strong advocate of the war posed a ticklish problem. Scott had recovered sufficiently to be stumping the state on crutches. He spoke at war meetings, urging young men to enlist and condemning the seditious statements of "Copperhead" Clement Vallandigham. Scott's popularity and his condemnation of Vallandigham worried Seymour, for both he and Vallandigham were Democrats who held similar antiwar views. The governor sent an emissary to query Scott. If Scott would support the governor in his coming election, Seymour would grant Scott his commission. Scott refused. The governor's actions only served to earn him a committed adversary. Scott canvassed a previously Democratic township in Genesee County for Reuben E. Fenton, the Republican candidate for governor. Fenton carried the township and the election. After his inauguration, Fenton offered Scott his commission, but the young clergyman declined. The two wounds in his right leg were still not healed, and the war was almost over. Scott had been officially mustered out of the service on September 23, 1864. In total, he had been wounded five times during the war, twice severely, and he had earned the sobriquet of "the fighting parson." He would carry his wounds for the rest of his life, but he would not nurse them. It is a measure of the man that the people he met in his daily life did not know of the constant pain he endured. Winfield Scott served his country well. Now it was time to get on with life, to rededicate his life in service to his God and his fellowman. He had been through the valley of death. It was time to return to the land of the living.

CHAPTER III

Missionary to Kansas

On December 22, 1864, Winfield Scott was appointed missionary to Kansas by the board of the American Baptist Home Mission Society. Whether compelled by a restlessness that affects men after a war or whether pulled by a force that had gripped many another Scott, the young pastor chose to make his life beyond the Mississippi. He might have chosen to serve his God in a comfortable pastorate in the East, but he did not. He chose the rigorous course of becoming a Baptist missionary, and the Home Mission Board voted to pay his expenses to Kansas. Although not specifically mentioned by Scott, here is yet another reason he declined his colonel's commission. He had already committed himself to another authority.

After the Civil War, the various Protestant denominations in the United States sought to expand their influence and memberships.[1] With the immediate goal of emancipation finally achieved, they turned their sights to new horizons. The American West, where vacant territory was being rapidly settled, appeared particularly promising. Few churches had yet ventured onto the frontier, but now home mission boards were established, and they dispatched missionaries to organize congregations and build churches. These missionaries sought to convert the uninitiated and to bring back into the fold those who had fallen away from the faith while living on the frontier. They built churches on or near Indian reservations to introduce the tenets of Christianity to the Native American. They took up cudgels against the saloon, the gambling hall, and the bordello in order to save man for his own sake and for God's work. It was an ambitious undertaking, and the Reverend Winfield Scott was in the vanguard of the movement.

In May 1864 two small Baptist congregations in Leavenworth, Kansas, totaling twenty-eight members, had united to form the "Baptist Church and Society, Leavenworth." They had tried several times to secure a regular preacher, but to no avail. A Sunday school, existing under trying conditions, was all that remained when they received a letter from the Home Mission Board recommending Winfield Scott as their pastor. To allow the congregation an opportunity to take the measure of the young preacher, the matter of issuing an invitation to become their pastor was held in abeyance until Scott arrived in Kansas.

When the twenty-eight-year-old minister and his wife stepped off a Missouri River steamboat in mid-January 1865, they viewed a frontier town in transition. At its zenith in the late 1850s, Leavenworth had been one of the major gateways for the Santa Fe trail, the Colorado and Utah goldfields, and the military posts of the West. In 1865, however, Leavenworth was being rapidly eclipsed by Kansas City, Missouri, as the commercial center of the Missouri Valley. Having been bypassed in 1863 as the eastern terminus of the first transcontinental railroad, Leavenworth in 1865 was desperately maneuvering to secure rail connections. It was still, by far, the largest town in Kansas with a population of twenty-five thousand, and it would remain so for some time. For a while longer it would also remain the major distribution point for the Santa Fe trade and the forts of the Great Plains, but Leavenworth had seen its finer frontier days.[2] What Scott and his wife viewed, then, was a community of acute contrasts. Here were found the accoutrements of civilized society beside the vestiges of the frontier, a bustling community with grand aspirations and a dwindling economic base. Leavenworth would provide a challenging setting for the work of the young preacher from the East.

It did not take long for the Leavenworth Baptists to reach a decision concerning Pastor Scott. On Sunday, January 29, 1865, a motion to call him to the pulpit carried unanimously. He received a yearly salary of $1,500, with his congregation supplying $800 and the Home Mission Society the balance. After Scott accepted the call, a discussion ensued on the "propriety" of building a church in the coming months. It appeared from the expressions of opinion that the question would take a great deal more thought and discussion. A special meeting was called for mid-March.

In the meantime, a call for aid went out to the community. C. P. Jenks, the church secretary, did not mince words in a letter to the local newspapers. He traced the history of the Leavenworth Baptists and heralded the new era marked by the coming of Pastor Scott. He stated that Scott was a diligent young man who meant to see God's work and the Baptist denomination flourish in Leavenworth. But, Jenks contin-

Fifth Street, Leavenworth, 1867. (Kansas State Historical Society)

ued, the young clergyman should not be permitted to do this work alone. He asked for the support of those who wished to see the Baptists succeed. He called on those Baptists who had not joined this congregation to do so now. To all he flatly stated, "Now is the time; we want all your time, influence or money." Whether or not community aid was forthcoming probably had little effect on the decision of the small Baptist congregation to build a church. They had been without a house of worship and a pastor for some time. Now they had an energetic pastor, and his enthusiasm was contagious. With high hopes, they decided to build the First Baptist Church of Leavenworth. They would have their own house of worship. C. B. Clarke, a St. Louis architect, was engaged, and ambitious plans for a magnificent edifice were drawn up. Winfield Scott and his congregation of nineteen had made a new beginning.

"Shall we gather at the river" was no choral metaphor for Scott and his hardy group as he baptized his first new members in the Missouri River on April 2, 1865. The work of building a congregation and a church edifice had begun in earnest. Baptist socials were held every Wednesday evening at a member's home. Naturally, guests were encouraged, and the newspaper articles detailing time and place invited "all friends" to join the festivities. To set the pattern of fellowship, the good pastor held the first social in his own home.

To build up his congregation, Scott used another standard tool, the monthly Sunday school concert. It was a showcase for the church and demonstrated the quality of religious education maintained by the Baptists. The children sang hymns and recited their lessons from the previous month. Usually one or two short addresses by visiting dignitaries and perhaps an adult soloist completed the program. Long before radio and television, Sunday evenings could hang heavily on the mind, and concerts of this kind were a welcome respite for those so inclined. Light entertainment also helped bring new members into the church. In the spring of 1865 the tragic death of President Abraham Lincoln necessarily postponed the Sunday school concert. Instead of welcoming new friends to the first in a series of enjoyable Sunday evening concerts, Scott spoke at a memorial service at Laing's Hall. For such a newcomer to be asked to help enunciate the collective grief of the community was a signal honor.

The rest of 1865 must have passed quickly for Winfield Scott and his wife. Sunday school concerts, picnics, socials, and church suppers came one after another. The young clergyman was called upon to say the prayers for Leavenworth's Fourth of July celebration, and in the fall he volunteered to teach history to the students of Leavenworth High School. The annual Sunday school outing, a fixture of many

Leavenworth churches, saw the Scotts chaperoning an interesting excursion. Since Leavenworth, as yet, had no railroad, and since the Missouri River was the main avenue for transportation, the First Baptist Church of Leavenworth chartered the river steamer *Emilie* to take them downstream to a shady grove for their picnic. Tickets were fifty cents for adults and twenty-five cents for children. The public was cordially invited, and people came by the score. They thronged the decks, the cabins, and even the wheelhouse, and young and old enjoyed the daylong outing. In addition to being a time of good fellowship for the congregation and an opportunity to recruit new members, the picnic helped raise money for the building fund. From this and all other activities, $17,500 was raised that first year. In November the cornerstone was laid, and workmen completed thirteen feet of vertical brickwork and installed a temporary roof. Even with this rapid progress, the church remained far from ready for occupancy.

Helen Scott busied herself that year making preparations for the arrival of their first child. The newest member of the congregation was a baby girl whom they named Minnie. Since the Scott family had a tradition of naming their sons and daughters after the children's uncles and aunts, it is likely that Minnie was named for Winfield's sister Minerva. In any event, the congregation, cognizant of the financial strain a new baby places on a young couple just starting out, gave Scott a donation party the week after the cornerstone laying. A $1,500 salary and an annual Civil War pension of $180 did not render the Scotts destitute, but to make ends meet on $140 per month required great imagination on the part of a minister's wife. She constantly entertained members of the congregation, visiting missionaries, and ladies' aid groups; all at a time when coffee sold for $.50 a pound, tea for $2.50 a pound, and flour for $10.00 a hundredweight. The Scotts greatly appreciated every bit of financial help.

The church found itself in a more straitened financial condition, however, because $17,500 did not cover even a third of the total building and furnishing costs. The blueprints for the First Baptist Church called for a 160-foot clock tower, solid black walnut pews, stained glass windows, ten gas chandeliers, and a main auditorium seating more than one thousand people. The total cost amounted to over $60,000. Construction came to a halt as the Baptists faced a worsening economic climate and stiff competition for dollars.

As a means of securing vital rail connections, Leavenworth issued $500,000 in bonds during 1865 to aid in the construction of railroads. Leavenworth County followed suit issuing $1,050,000 in bonds. This funding was undertaken in addition to the $250,000 in bonds issued in 1864, also for railroad construction. To pay the interest on this rapidly

Cathedral of the Immaculate Conception under construction in Leavenworth, 1867. (Kansas State Historical Society)

Leavenworth High School under construction, 1867. (Kansas State Historical Society)

expanding debt, taxes were raised. Unfortunately, they were raised during a period of declining commerce. Kansas City was drawing trade away from Leavenworth, and the end of the Civil War brought a sharp drop in commodity prices.[3] In addition to the bleak economic picture, the Baptists faced the uncomfortable fact that they were not alone in soliciting funds for a new building. Most of the Protestant churches of Leavenworth decided to build new houses of worship after the war, with more imposing brick edifices replacing the frame structures of territorial days. This flurry of new construction split the community money pie into increasingly smaller pieces.

In the competition for souls, the Baptists faced an even more formidable adversary in their Roman Catholic brethren. Begun before the Civil War ended, the Cathedral of the Immaculate Conception was then under construction in Leavenworth, and consciously or unconsciously, it served as a goad to the resourcefulness of the Baptists. In 1850 Pope Pius IX had appointed Bishop Jean Baptiste Miege as Vicar Apostolic of the Indian Territory, and in 1855 the Bishop visited Leavenworth, making it his permanent home. Funds to construct a cathedral to grace the Bishop's field were raised primarily in France and South America, and when it was completed, the cathedral cost close to a quarter million dollars.[4] Had it not been for the cathedral, it is debatable whether the Baptists would have contemplated such an imposing structure of their own.

Finally, the Leavenworth Board of Education planned to erect a substantial four-story, brick high school costing approximately $50,000. Railroad, church, and civic projects seemingly conspired to make the fund-raising efforts of the tiny Baptist congregation incredibly difficult. They had chosen to expend a large sum of money at a time when money was becoming increasingly dear, and the limited amount of cash had an increasing number of calls on its use. As a result, funds slowed to a trickle, and the Leavenworth Baptists continued to rely on the hospitality of their neighbors.

The beginning of 1866 saw renewed efforts to raise funds. With the money-well seemingly dry in Leavenworth, Scott decided to look elsewhere for donations. He wrote the Home Mission Board with a request that they appoint another of their missionaries in Kansas, the Reverend H. K. Stimson, as his church's agent to solicit funds in the East. The Board consented, and the Reverend Stimson, a seasoned Baptist veteran thirty-three years Scott's senior, left Kansas in early February. For nine months he spoke to Baptist associations from Chicago to Boston. In large cities and small towns he raised over $1,300 and gained innumerable pledges to the Leavenworth building fund by filling the pulpits of ministers on vacation. At home Scott and his congregation bid farewell to the Congregational Church and hired Laing's Hall for Sunday services. If only for a few hours every Sunday, the rented auditorium was their own place of worship.

In early June 1866 the First Baptist Church of Leavenworth hosted the seventh annual meeting of the Baptist State Convention. Such an undertaking entailed considerable work and expense, as the host church had to supply not only food and lodging for all the delegates but also hay for the horses of their guests. The honor for the young church, however, was worth the expense, and their pastor received the additional personal recognition of being elected secretary of the executive board. Coming fast on the heels of the convention, the ladies of the congregation held a strawberry festival to raise money for the building fund. It seems the ladies of Scott's congregation received barely a moment's pause. They worked tirelessly on behalf of their church.

The steamer *Emilie* was once again secured for the summer's Sunday school outing, and a brass band came along to add gaiety to the occasion. In the middle of the afternoon a thunderstorm gathered rapidly and sent the picnickers running for cover in Parkville, a small settlement nearby. When the storm had passed, Scott assembled the children, and, accompanied by the brass band, they serenaded the townspeople. Wherever and whenever he could, the enthusiastic young preacher promoted the cause of his church.

The money from the strawberry festival, the summer outing, and the Reverend Stimson's efforts proved sufficient for construction to begin again, and the supports for the second story were soon installed. Money needs, however, seemed never ending, and in September Scott requested and received a leave of absence to solicit funds in the Boston area. He traveled in the Northeast for several months and, with the help of Deacon J. W. Converse and Deacon H. S. Chase of Boston, raised several thousand dollars. Despite all these efforts, the Leavenworth Baptists reached only a little more than one-third of their goal. It was a discouraging situation for even the most resolute, but Pastor Scott kept the faith and carried his congregation with him.

The next several years consisted of a succession of peaks and valleys for Winfield Scott and his congregation. The Opera House, the Christian Church, and the German Methodist Church served as additional havens for the First Baptist Church. The baptismal font in the basement of the new church was finally ready in March of 1867, and the frontier practice of baptism in the river came to an end.

By this time the Baptist Sunday school was a successful institution, having an average weekly attendance of 174 "scholars." Thirteen thousand dollars was raised in 1867, and in July twenty masons went back to work. The twin towers of the church began to rise above the prairie landscape, and the Leavenworth *Times* related that the church would be finished by fall. The strain of three years of nonstop fund raising, traveling, and preaching finally caught up with Scott in the fall of 1867. It is not known what felled him, but by early November, he was reported on the mend. And still the church remained unfinished. The fall came and went without an announcement of success.

In 1868 Scott and his congregation moved into the basement of the new church. After three years work, they at last had their own roof over their heads. The Scotts' second daughter Helen was born that year, and the family moved to the suburbs, a section of northwestern Leavenworth known as Pilot Knob. On his six-acre parcel Scott took up dairying and potato farming to supplement his income and to re-establish his contact with the land. The high-grade milk from his Jersey cows helped nourish his growing daughters, and the potatoes helped feed the widows and orphans in his care.

In 1869 Scott arranged a series of six lectures as another means of fund raising. For one of the programs he enlisted the aid of old friend and roommate David H. Robinson, professor of Latin language and literature at the University of Kansas at Lawrence. Robinson's journey to Leavenworth gave the two Rochester alumni a chance to exchange news about old friends and acquaintances. Scott also enlisted Isaac S. Kalloch, controversial Baptist minister, town founder, and railroad promoter, to deliver a lecture. Kalloch and Scott would be associated for many years, with Scott later working under Kalloch in California. The relationship seemed to bring turbulence to Scott's life, but now the Baptist veteran with "the golden voice" was helping the young preacher raise money. By the end of that summer Scott had been elected president of the Baptist State Convention, and the Baptists of Chicago had donated to the building fund. Yet in spite of continuing and unceasing efforts, the church remained incomplete.

In addition to his work in Leavenworth, Scott took an interest in the larger Baptist cause in Kansas. In early 1869 he and Brother Stimson suggested to their Baptist brethren assembled at LaNape that a portable meetinghouse was needed to conduct the Baptist ministry on the plains of Kansas. The physical elements–dust,wind, and rain–made holding meetings on the open plains difficult. Having observed the utility of huge tents during their army days, the two ministers suggested that the Baptists secure one for their missionary labors. In the small towns of Kansas where there were no halls sufficiently large to hold religious revivals, meetings could be brought indoors through the use of a tent. The idea was enthusiastically endorsed, and Brother Stimson was dispatched to the East to solicit funds for the building of the "Baptist Tabernacle for Kansas." Having been successful on the eastern seaboard, Stimson journeyed to Chicago to have the "Tabernacle" constructed.

Stimson's enthusiasm for the project resulted in a tent that could seat sixteen hundred comfortably and twenty-five hundred if the weather was not too sultry. The Chicago, Burlington and Quincy and the Hannibal and St. Joseph railroads volunteered their lines to move the huge tent to Leavenworth during the summer of 1869. There, amid derisive catcalls about the Baptists going into the circus business, Scott and Stimson had the "Baptist Tabernacle" erected for its dedication to God's work. It may have been much too large for most of the small communities in Kansas where it was to be used, but Winfield Scott would put it to good use in his role of missionary for the convention and evangelist for Kansas.

In the spring of 1870 the Reverend Mr. Scott resigned his pastorate in Leavenworth. The long awaited completion of the First Baptist Church was in sight; his responsibility had been fulfilled. At the urging of the Baptist State Convention and the Home Mission Society, Scott became a general missionary for Kansas. For nine months, from May 1, 1870, to January 20, 1871, he traveled the state, logging by his own reckoning 6,682 miles. In towns such as Olathe, Baxter Springs, and La Cygne, which had no Baptist church, Scott set up the "Baptist Tabernacle" and held meetings to raise money to build one. In small hamlets all across Kansas, he raised $4,750 with which to build new churches and pay off old debts. He preached 171 sermons and delivered 19 addresses in those nine months. He attended 75 prayer meetings in his capacity as evangelist for Kansas and made 700 visitations to the sick, the destitute, and the lonely. The figures cited here are Scott's, and they are a testament to his energy and dedication. But that is not all. In addition, he organized two churches and found the time to aid Brother Post at Fort Scott and Brother Baldwin at Mound City in their pastoral labors.

One of the churches Scott organized was in a small town in Cowley County, not far from the border of the Indian Territory. Legend has it that the town was originally named Legonda, although that name had not been formally approved by the settlers. To entice his wife to leave Leavenworth, W. W. Andrews promised her that she could name the new town. Being a loyal member of Pastor Scott's congregation, she wanted to name the town Winfield in his honor. Mrs. Andrews most likely chose Scott's given name, as there was already a Fort Scott, Kansas, named after General Winfield Scott. The advocates of the different names reportedly held an election to decide the matter. To assure her new home the name Winfield, Mrs. Andrews intimated that she tampered with the ballots during the dancing that followed.[5]

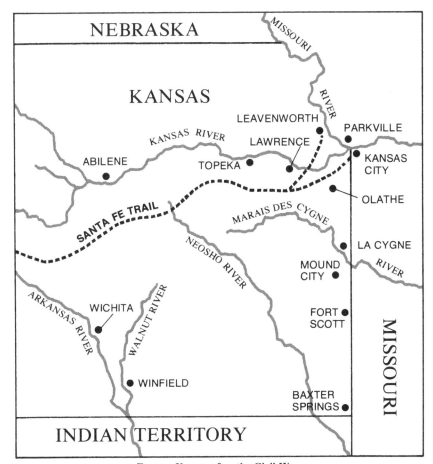

Eastern Kansas after the Civil War

Another version of the story is that Scott jokingly told the towns-people that if they would name their village for him, he would build them a church. Regardless of how the town received its name, the church was founded when Scott, on a hunting trip in the area, held a series of religious services in the unfinished store of A. H. Green. Planks were laid over the floor joists for pews, and a dry-goods box served as the pulpit. After the services on November 27, 1870, Scott called a meeting, and eleven individuals met to organize a Baptist congregation. With Scott's assistance, they formed the First Baptist Church of Winfield, Kansas.

Scott ceased his labors as missionary after only nine months, be-cause the Baptist Convention ran out of money. "Feeling unable and unwilling to labor without provision to meet expenses," Scott laid aside

First Baptist Church of Leavenworth, at the corner of Sixth Street and Seneca, with interior view. (First Baptist Church of Leavenworth)

his missionary work and prepared to dedicate the First Baptist Church of Leavenworth. The newly completed building was dedicated February 26, 1871, on Winfield Scott's thirty-fourth birthday. Although Scott had resigned in April 1870, his congregation had voted not to make the resignation official until after the dedication. They knew the First Baptist Church of Leavenworth, all 800,000 bricks, was Winfield Scott's church, and he deserved the honor of being its pastor upon its dedication. It stood as a remarkable achievement for Scott and his congregation, now 250 strong. In spite of overwhelming difficulties and disappointments, the "Baptist Church and Society, Leavenworth," with their pastor's example to guide them, had persevered. A church resolution, passed December 31, 1869, eloquently expresses the feelings of the congregation for their pastor:

> *Resolved,* That we are under special obligations to our pastor, Rev. Winfield Scott, for his untiring zeal and persistent efforts in advancing our interest regardless of his own, and that we do now heartily acknowledge our appreciation of his services, and extend to him our sincere thanks.
>
> He has labored to build our Bethel most cheerfully and assiduously amid discouragements and burdens that few could bear, and in all his trials and embarrassments, being an example to his flock and the world of unwavering faith in God's promise, when nearly all other hearts failed. He trusted in God and has not been disappointed. While many others have given most liberally and cheerfully, he has often gone beyond duty, giving all he had or could acquire, till, in addition to his other efforts, he has given forty-five hundred dollars, a sum considerably larger than he has received from the church for his pastoral services while among us, and
>
> *Resolved,* That we will ever gratefully remember his self-sacrificing labors to ensure us a sanctuary of our own in which to worship the Lord our God, and render Him thanks and praise for His goodness and mercy to us.

At about this same time, the Kansas legislature passed an appropriations bill funding the Kansas Immigration Society. For many years immigrants had been streaming into Kansas at an ever-increasing pace, while efforts to develop a comprehensive, state-funded immigration plan fell on deaf ears in Topeka. Individuals and ad hoc groups had tried to stimulate and promote immigration to Kansas with their personal funds. One novel approach to disseminate promotional literature had been to print the answers to the most frequently asked questions about Kansas on the back of two-page note paper. The note paper sold for just a bit more than plain paper, but public-spirited Kansans bought it to write letters home. In this ingenious way, a great deal of Kansas propaganda reached the East at minimal expense to the Kansas boosters. By 1871, however, Kansas hospitality was receiving a tarnished reputation. Unscrupulous innkeepers, cafe owners, and railway agents were gouging unsuspecting immigrants who were seeking the promised land in Kansas. The legislature finally awoke to the situation and established the Kansas Immigration Society with Winfield Scott as general superintendent.

Scott was eminently qualified for this position. In the course of his missionary labors, he had traveled extensively throughout Kansas, and it was inevitable that he had come in contact with a goodly proportion of the state's innkeepers, stationmasters, landowners, and bankers. In short, he had rubbed shoulders with those people whose business it was to promote Kansas. In addition, his reputation as a "wide-awake" Christian salesman had been well established throughout Kansas. He was a natural choice for the position.

The society set up its general headquarters in Leavenworth and soon was processing a steady stream of correspondence. Plans were made to exhibit Kansas products at state fairs in the East. The secretary of the society secured the necessary maps to show the eager immigrant what private and government land was still available in Kansas. Satellite offices were planned about the state, and the society reached agreements with the railroads to assure immigrants bound for Kansas of discount first-class railway accommodations. The society also signed contracts with at least one inn, boardinghouse, or hotel in every Kansas town to supply immigrants with decent meals and lodgings at reasonable prices. Superintendent Scott toured the East that winter and spring, and during the summer of 1871 forty thousand immigrants came to Kansas. Many of them would have come without the efforts of Winfield Scott and the Kansas Immigration Society, but at least their journey was greatly eased.

Winfield Scott had come to Leavenworth as a novice in the ways of the West. With his congregation, he built a church that was the pride and joy of both the Kansas Baptists and the city in which it stood. As a Baptist missionary and the superintendent of immigration, he helped build Kansas both literally and figuratively. In his own way, he helped make the Kansas that he promoted. Seven years of effort were invested, and it proved a mutually beneficial experience. With his pastorate in Kansas completed, Winfield Scott was assigned by the board of the Home Mission Society to pick up the traces in Colorado.

CHAPTER IV

On the Slopes of the Rockies

The Reverend Winfield Scott reached Denver in October 1871. The little town on the banks of Cherry Creek was growing rapidly. Both the Denver Pacific and the Kansas Pacific railroads had reached Denver during the summer of 1870, and by the end of 1871 perhaps ten thousand people made Denver their home. The Denver Baptists, however, were not participating in the community's growth, and Scott's success in Kansas interested them. They admired the enthusiastic energy he brought to building congregations, and, more important, they were in dire need of his ability to build churches.

Since December 1866 the First Baptist Church of Denver had been worshiping in what was known locally as the "Holy Dug-Out." It had been started with great hopes, but by the time the basement was excavated and the first four feet of wall above ground were completed, the congregation ran out of money. A roof was attached to this structure, which then resembled the sod houses of the plains, and here the First Baptist Church of Denver worshiped until Pastor Scott arrived.[1] Before they extended an invitation to Scott to become their pastor, the Denver Baptists decided to exercise their prerogative of taking the measure of the new preacher. The Denver Bible Society, however, had no doubt that Scott would be called to the pulpit, and on October 17, 1871, its members elected him a vice-president. Scott did some investigating of his own during the last months of 1871 and decided that Denver was of sufficient size and liberality to justify a major building effort by the Baptists.

On January 1, 1872, Winfield Scott received the call to the pulpit of the First Baptist Church and began at once to raise the money needed to build a new house of worship. A busy week followed for Scott, for the next day he was elected chaplain to the upper house of the ninth annual session of the Colorado Territorial Legislature. On that opening day of the legislative session, the first two-mile section of track of the Denver Horse Railway Company opened for business. The legislators received a free ride over the route as part of the formal opening,[2] and in his official capacity Chaplain Scott very likely went along for the ride. Just the previous January, Denver had been lighted with gas, and now the inauguration of street railway service had become a reality. Little wonder that Scott felt Denver ready to contribute toward a suitable Baptist church.

To Scott the "Holy Dug-Out" represented a major obstacle to enlarging the congregation and to raising building funds. In a letter to a friend, he expressed his concern.

> They have been worshipping for the past few years in the meanest place for a decent city I ever saw. A stone basement 40x70 and 9 feet high; with only four feet above ground. The roof was of rough boards; the inside was whitewashed upon the naked stone walls; cheap board seats with back breakers attached, served as stools of penance; the whole place being sufficiently dismal to drive all but the most faithful to other congregations, whose pleasant and comfortable churches cause this one to be shunned by all except those who have good health, Baptist backbone, and sufficient nerve and faith to face, enter and carry this pit. We are saved by faith.[3]

It was said that toads hopped about during the services, and that mice and rats were often the most attentive listeners. Another Baptist preacher, A. H. Burlingham of St. Louis, who occasionally filled the Denver pulpit, echoed Scott's sentiments. "The church holds services in a dilapidated owl and bat kind of basement. Nobody but a saint, a very pious and obstinate Baptist saint, would go into that dugout." Rather than test the piety of his forty-member congregation any longer than necessary, Scott decided to employ a measure from his Kansas days. In early June 1872 he obtained a tent capable of seating several hundred people and moved his congregation out of the "Holy Dug-Out."

From the time of his arrival in Denver, Scott worked to obtain a good location for the new church "more in keeping with the improved state of civilization and progress in that thriving city." The first pastor of the Denver church had had, like Scott, a good eye for business and had purchased a large tract at the intersection of Eighteenth and Curtis during his stay in Denver. The ultimate legatees of that property were the American Baptist Home Mission Society and the American Baptist Missionary Union. Scott worked through two prominent Baptist leaders, Martin B. Anderson and E. J. Goodspeed, to obtain four lots from

Denver in the early 1870s. (Denver Public Library, Western History Department)

the larger property. Deacon Francis Gallup, an 1864 charter member of the church, had been caretaker of those lands since 1867, both chasing off claim jumpers and paying $2,000 in taxes out of his own pocket. In recognition of his services to these two organizations, the four lots, worth $4,000, were deeded to Deacon Gallup. He, in turn, donated the lots to the church, and the first major hurdle was cleared. In August the Baptists broke ground on the lots, just three blocks from the "Holy Dug-Out," and construction began.[4]

As previously noted, the Sunday school program of the Baptist church played an important role in Scott's ministry. In Leavenworth the Baptist concert had been a showcase for the church, and so it would become in Denver. Scott brought the concept with him, and the first Sunday concert of the First Baptist Church of Denver took place in mid-May 1872. As an indication of the importance he placed on the program, Pastor Scott taught Sunday school that first year in addition to his ministerial and fund-raising duties. Helen Scott also became involved as a teacher in 1874. The special summer outing was another Sunday school activity incorporated into Scott's Denver ministry. His first summer in Colorado, the children received a trip to the top of the Continental Divide on the Denver and Rio Grande Railroad, and each summer thereafter the members of the Baptist Sunday school enjoyed an outing in the country.

Once settled in Denver, Scott began dairy farming again with a herd of fifteen Jersey cows. He became an active member of the Colorado Stock Growers' Association and entered into a dairy partnership with Andrew Ward and Farley Porter. Dairying, however, was not the only business in which Scott became involved. He joined with six Baptist brethren to form the Idaho Springs Hotel, Manufacturing and Mining Company in February 1873. Idaho Springs was a small mining and health resort community situated high in the Rocky Mountains west of Denver. The area had been the site of an early Colorado gold discovery in 1859, and the following year miners established a town near the diggings. As early as 1868, health seekers came to enjoy the benefits of the hot soda springs located there, and a huge frame bathhouse catered to their needs. In 1869 the Rock Island House, containing only three rooms but billed preposterously as the "most pretentious hostelry in town," was built to serve the increasing numbers of tourists coming to the area.[5] Soon the Colorado Central, a narrow gauge railroad, reached Idaho Springs to bring in the tourists and take out the ore. As word of the alleged medicinal value of the springs spread, there was talk of building another rail line, the Denver, Georgetown and Utah, through Idaho Springs.[6] It is little wonder that Scott and his associates felt it a propitious time to build another hotel at the Springs. They also planned to develop a park and to engage in mining. Unfortunately, not much else is known of this venture, but it appears the Baptist brethren had more enthusiasm than expertise. It is also quite possible that the national business panic of September 1873 ruined any chance of success. Of these ambitious efforts Scott remarked in later years that he had "tried to set the Lord up in business, but it was a grand failure."

By October 1872 the congregation had grown to ninety-four members. Construction had proceeded apace, and on October 15, the cornerstone was laid with appropriate ceremony. In his remarks on that happy occasion, Scott espoused a philosophy of religion that explains, to a certain extent, his popularity as a minister. In part, he said,

> Thank God, the pulpit is no longer considered so sacred that dogmatism therein can take the place of reason; that credulity can be demanded therein of the people, instead of an intelligent faith. . . . The pulpit is considered a platform, where a man meets his fellow men; where reason is pitted against reason; where judgement meets judgement; where instruction given is subject to criticism and questioning. . . . The pulpit is no longer the controller of conscience, but is simply the instructor of conscience. . . . Thus the pulpit is to be made a help to men to live here, as well as hereafter. . . . No relation in life, nor related truth, is to be ignored; but all questions that relate to the well being of man, in all of his relations, whether at home, in social society, connected with the state, or referring to the kingdom to come. . . .
>
> We build, and intend to dedicate, this temple to the interests of man as well as to God. We build this for the earth, as well as for heaven; for man that he may be sought, and saved, and brought to God; for earth, that it may be blessed and purified and fitted for heaven.

In these words of Pastor Scott are heard the stirrings of a movement known in the history of American Protestantism as the social gospel. His thoughts convey the essence of what a small group of progressive Protestant clergymen were advocating as a means of coping with the problems related to a burgeoning, urban, industrial society. Putting aside that part of Protestant orthodoxy that was solely concerned with man's life in the hereafter, they sought to deal with man and his problems in this life. Their early preaching of a more humanistic Christianity laid the intellectual groundwork for the fully developed social gospel of Washington Gladden and Walter Rauschenbusch.[7]

Scott and a legion of other clergymen had always preached against the evils of gambling, but Scott, addressing himself to this problem, took a novel approach in keeping with his philosophy of the pulpit as an open platform. He invited the "knights of the green cloth" to his Denver church to judge for themselves whether he was evenhanded in dealing with the situation. Many came to Scott's service and went away with the opinion that he had fairly stated their case.

Another method the clergy employed in dealing with man's problems in this world was to support the expansion of the YMCA and its four-point program of physical, educational, social, and religious endeavors. Scott was in the mainstream of progressive Protestant clergy in this regard also, and he offered his aid in the organization of the Denver YMCA. Being a practical businessman, he understood the growing national fascination with business, technology, and industry. His sermons were laced with business themes and the relationship of good business and Christianity. In both word and deed, the Reverend

First Baptist Church of Denver, Eighteenth Street and Curtis. (Denver Public Library, Western History Department)

Winfield Scott is a good example of the Protestant clergyman who came to embrace the early social gospel.

By February 1873 with the furnace installed, the roof finished, and the baptistry ready to receive its first convert, the church at Eighteenth and Curtis was sufficiently completed to be occupied. With much rejoicing, the congregation said good-bye to its drafty tent, moved into the new tabernacle, and within three months welcomed seventy-five new members. In August the church was dedicated with A. H. Burlingham of St. Louis preaching the sermon. The metamorphosis of the First Baptist Church truly amazed Burlingham:

> Such a resurrection I scarcely ever saw before. The Baptist cause is looking up. They stand even with any other church in this city. Thanks to God first and thanks to Rev. Winfield Scott second. He has honesty, pluck, wisdom, common sense and piety, and does not propose to fail in what he undertakes.

About his congregation's successful efforts to build a church, Scott himself was ebullient:

> We lifted until we could see stars, sledded on dry ground, tugged and pulled until we broke the traces and nearly went wild and blind in trying to move our load. The little church was united and in blood earnest. We never lost one ounce of the effect of our efforts through friction. There was absolutely one mind, one will and one wish; everyone was hopeful and earnest. Everyone said to his neighbor "be of good courage." We pushed for victory from the start.

The new building of the Denver Baptists cost $12,000 and contained the first pipe organ west of the Missouri River.[8]

Wherever he went Winfield Scott brought music to his churches; it was an important part of his ministry. He believed that music uplifted the spirit equally as much as sermon or prayer, so bringing a $3,600 organ to the slopes of the Rockies was a practical matter for Pastor Scott. Congregational singing opened the heart and made one receptive to the preacher's words, and congregational singing was at its finest with a booming organ behind it. The organ and a parsonage swelled the total cost of the church, and although it saddled them with additional debt, the affairs of the Denver Baptists were looking up.

Scott maintained close ties with the young Colorado Stock Growers' Association. On its behalf he made a special trip to Lawrence, Kansas, where he secured the loan of two stallions to help improve the breed of trotting horses in Colorado. He was also an association delegate to the Kansas City Pork Packers' and Stock Men's Convention in the fall of 1873. Scott's acceptance and position in the growers' association was not an honorary one, for he was a dedicated dairyman. He presented papers on dairying at the annual growers' convention, and, at the territorial fair in July 1874, Scott's Jersey cows and bulls won six blue ribbons. If innkeeping and mining were not his forte, dairy farming seemed to be, and in the context of Scott family traditions, that was as it should be.

By October 1874 the First Baptist Church of Denver boasted 198 members and stood proudly on its own solid foundation. Membership had increased fivefold since the arrival of Pastor Scott. He had become one of the most popular ministers in Denver, because he "never minced words and his original eloquence and straight-forward manner delighted his congregations."[9] Winfield Scott had accomplished what he had been asked to accomplish. His appointment to Denver by the Home Mission Board expired January 1, 1875, but Scott stayed on a few months longer. In April he resigned his pastorate with a view to settling his personal affairs in Denver, and the Reverend T. W. Greene, an associate from Kansas days, took over the minister's duties as pastoral supply. Greene had been on his way to San Francisco to assume the editorial management of the *Evangel,* the Baptist news-paper of the Pacific Coast, but his good offices were needed in Denver for a brief time. Greene remained in Denver six months, and both he and Scott bade farewell to the First Baptist Church of Denver on the same Sunday in October 1875. They were on their way to California.

CHAPTER V

California Odyssey

Winfield Scott arrived in California in October 1875, less than one month after the failure of William C. Ralston's Bank of California. Ralston had overextended his San Francisco bank in mining ventures on the Comstock Lode, and the bank closed its doors when the depression following the Panic of 1873 eventually forced major reductions in the mining, smelting, and sale of silver. Bankruptcies, the temporary closing of almost every bank in California, serious unemployment, and the permanent closing of the Temple and Workman Bank in Los Angeles followed in the wake of Ralston's ruin.[1] It had taken two years for the Panic of 1873 to hit California, and its impact changed the course of the thirty-eight-year-old Scott's life and sent him on a California odyssey.

Winfield Scott reportedly came to California to serve as assistant pastor to Isaac S. Kalloch,[2] but a committee to which Kalloch belonged soon appointed Scott as centennial financial agent for California College. Run by the California Baptists at Vacaville, about forty-five miles northeast of San Francisco, California College offered a four-year, coeducational, liberal arts program and specialized in ministerial training.[3] The school chronically experienced severe financial problems and hoped to capitalize on the upcoming United States Centennial to improve its anemic financial condition. As their centennial tribute, the Baptists of the United States pledged themselves to raise $5 million for education, and it became Scott's job as centennial financial agent to secure for the school as much of California's pledge as possible. Isaac Kalloch served as president of the board of trustees and helped select Scott for the financial agent's position. It appears he felt the school needed Scott's services more than he did.

Isaac S. Kalloch and Winfield Scott had become associates in Kansas. After leaving Boston and New York where both success and controversy had marked his pastorates, Kalloch moved on to Kansas, left the ministry, and engaged in land promotion, town building, newspaper publishing, and railroad construction. There again, controversy surrounded him, and one was either a strong supporter of the man or a vehement detractor. Scott stood as a Kalloch supporter, and Kalloch reciprocated in kind. Kalloch helped Scott with the building fund lecture series in 1869, and when Scott needed support on his Boston fundraising trip, Kalloch undoubtedly secured the aid of the deacons of his former congregation. Their generous assistance was immediately forthcoming. Before leaving Leavenworth for Denver, Scott sold his Jersey cows to Kalloch, who owned an extensive stock farm near Lawrence, and later, Scott returned from Denver to preach the installation sermon when Kalloch reentered the ministry as pastor of the First Baptist Church of Leavenworth. The two men had much in common, their Baptist ministry, their fund-raising and superior speaking abilities, and their interest in farming. They also differed in many ways. Kalloch was a large man, standing well over six feet and weighing 220 pounds. He enjoyed good bourbon, a stylish wardrobe, and fast horses.[4] Scott, in contrast, stood five foot six and weighed 147 pounds. He held strong temperance views and led a completely unpretentious life. Yet Winfield Scott remained a Kalloch supporter throughout Kalloch's tumultuous career. Kalloch, in return, played a key supporting role in Scott's six years in California. During those years Scott held a series of positions, "usually," he wrote, "straightening up and paying debts" for the churches he assisted. The one constant in this itinerant portion of his career became the backing, for better or for worse, of I. S. Kalloch.

In his position as financial agent for California College, Scott toured the state, speaking from Baptist pulpits. He did not want the job, believing someone familiar to California's Baptists would be more effective, but once persuaded, he plunged ahead with characteristic energy. In an open letter to the state's Baptists, he again revealed the fighting spirit that had assured his previous successes.

> God has made us a world by ourselves and now if we expect to be cultured and educated, and morally developed as we can be and ought to be, we must build up and endow and render permanent the great educational centers. . . . This is especially necessary for Baptists. Authors as we are of religious liberty, propagators and defenders of the great principle of which the world is now proud—the right of private judgement—and resting our religious faith upon the word of God, asking nothing of the world save an open Bible and a fair fight, it is especially necessary that the highest and broadest scholarship should be sought. . . . Here is work for California Baptists to do.

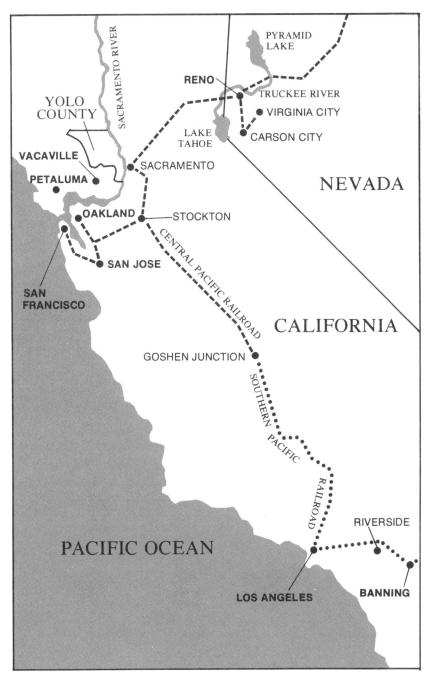

California and Nevada in the late 1870s

A bird's eye view of San Jose, 1875, the year Winfield Scott visited to dedicate the new Baptist Church. (The Bancroft Library)

Scott made his headquarters at the college in Vacaville, and when on campus, he lectured and preached to the student body. In late November 1875 he accompanied Kalloch to San Jose to dedicate the new Baptist church there. For a time in 1880, Scott would occupy this pulpit, but at the Sunday dedication, Kalloch preached the morning service, he conducted the evening service, and between them they raised nearly $4,000 with which to retire the church's indebtedness.

In early January 1876 Scott planned to move his base of operations to San Francisco, but his two daughters became seriously ill with typhoid fever, and he postponed the move. Two daughters of his uncle George W. Scott died of the disease in this outbreak, but Scott's daughters recovered. With the crisis past and his young cousins laid to rest, Scott resumed his fund raising, moved to San Francisco, and set up his headquarters in the office of the *Evangel*. Because T. W. Greene, who had come to California to edit the *Evangel*, had become president of California College instead, Isaac Kalloch continued to edit the newspaper, and it is likely that Kalloch used this opportunity to seek Scott's assistance with the paper's financial matters.

From his San Francisco base, Scott toured the northern counties of California soliciting funds for the endowment of California College. It is not known how much money he raised, but the bleak economic situation undoubtedly hampered his efforts, and during this period the school continued to have problems in meeting its financial obligations. When not in the field raising money, Scott lectured and preached in San Francisco. One Sunday he substituted for Kalloch in the Metropolitan Church in the morning and lectured to two thousand people at Dashaway Hall in the evening. In June he supplied the pulpit of the First Baptist Church of San Francisco while the Reverend E. B. Hulburt was on vacation, and on July 6, 1876, he became editor, publisher, and business manager of the *Evangel*.

Kalloch's detractors within the Baptist denomination on the Pacific Coast refused to support the *Evangel* as long as Kalloch served as editor, and support, both financial and moral, was something Kalloch wanted for the paper. He decided to step aside for an impartial editor who could rally the brethren to the newspaper's cause. Scott had expected to take over the business manager's job with a view to improving the paper's financial position, but suddenly he found himself center stage as editor and publisher as well. Said Kalloch in relinquishing the reins of power,

> The *Evangel*, including and after present issue, is in the hands and under the control, financially and editorially, of Rev. Winfield Scott, under the providence of God. Bro. Scott is not a pastor of any church, and therefore has no "entangling alliances." The *Evangel*, under his

care, cannot be suspected of being the organ, or he of being the favorite, of any of our churches. He can be the pastor of all of us, and the *Evangel* the paper for all of us.

In spite of his statement, Kalloch's foes suspected Scott of being Kalloch's man and continued to keep their hands in their pockets. Many others, however, cheerfully supported the new editor, and letters poured in congratulating Scott. Promising to represent the "whole denomination on the coast" and to stress a positive rather than negative attitude, Scott dusted off his college literary training and went to work. He offered special reduced subscription rates to help boost circulation. Where Kalloch had written with an acid pen, Scott tried conciliation and moderation in his editorials. Kalloch's detractors, however, wanted Scott to exhibit overt antagonism toward the controversial preacher as proof he was his own man, and this Scott would not do.

In mid-October, after several months of being a newspaper editor and supporting the paper out of his own pocket, Scott's personal funds began to run out, and he went before a meeting of the Baptist association to request $2,000 to keep the paper going. When associates who had promised to support him refused to allocate any funds, he knew he had not allayed their suspicions. Realizing that whatever he did to be fair would not be enough, and refusing to go into debt on the chance he might some day overcome suspicions, Scott resigned his position as editor of the *Evangel*. With no ill will toward the recalcitrant brethren, he moved on to become pastor of the First Baptist Church of Los Angeles.

The Baptists of Los Angeles, numbering probably less than a dozen members, had been without a pastor for over a year when Winfield Scott first visited them in September 1876. He had come to solicit aid for the *Evangel,* but soon after his arrival, he received the unanimous call of the congregation to become their pastor. Scott apparently held his decision in abeyance, but he stayed for two weeks and conducted a series of meetings to help the struggling church. Having no church building of their own, the Baptists shared a hall on Spring Street with the German Church, and there, on weekday evenings, Scott's meetings generated new interest in the Baptist cause. On Sundays Scott conducted morning services in the hall leased by the German Church and lectured in the evening in Union Hall, a second-floor meeting room over the Los Angeles Post Office. During the morning service on his first Sunday in Los Angeles, Scott baptized a group of converts from the evening meetings; already the future looked brighter.

Scott's call to the pulpit in Los Angeles contained the condition

A bird's eye view of Los Angeles, 1871. Although this scene depicts Los Angeles several years before Winfield Scott arrived to shepherd the First Baptist Church, the small, rural nature of the town did not change appreciably in the interim. (The Bancroft Library)

that the Home Mission Society of New York contribute $1,000 of his
$1,800 salary, but while Scott worked to gain backing for his paper, the
board of the Home Mission Society decided not to support his appointment to Los Angeles. The Los Angeles Baptists wanted Scott to come,
with or without support, and extended their call without aid from the
East. Realizing the futility of his efforts for the *Evangel,* Scott accepted
the invitation of the homeless church. It is not recorded what he was
paid, but Scott stayed with the congregation for fifteen months.

Socials, Sunday school concerts, and separate lectures for young
men and young women soon became a part of the Baptist ministry in
Los Angeles. The California missionary for the Baptist association,
C. A. Bateman, came down to assist Scott in gathering in new members, and within several weeks thirty-eight individuals joined the
church. Before Scott arrived in Los Angeles, the announcement of
Baptist services in the newspaper indicated they would be held in the
German Church, and the church directory contained two separate entries, one for the Baptist Church and one for the German Church. Soon
after Scott's arrival, the church announcements indicated Baptist services would be held in the Baptist Church, and the church directory
then contained one entry, "BAPTIST CHURCH—German Church."
Between the two small congregations, Scott's arrival tipped the scales
in favor of the Baptists, and they quite obviously assumed the lion's
share of the rent.

When Winfield Scott left San Francisco, Isaac Kalloch resumed
publishing the *Evangel* and ran the paper from his church. From Los
Angeles Scott aided his colleague for a time by contributing a column
for the *Evangel* entitled, "Home, Farm and Stock." The column included articles on farming written from Scott's personal experience,
articles reprinted from other periodicals, and even a poem or two ex-
toling motherhood, hearth, and home. At the same time Scott began a
small paper to promote the First Baptist Church of Los Angeles. He
called it *Our Church Banner* and intended the first, free run of five
thousand copies to reach every household in the Los Angeles area. San
Francisco, by comparison, had a population of approximately 200,000
people and reigned as California's queen city.

Despite a doubling in population during the 1870s, Los Angeles
remained a sleepy hamlet until the arrival from the north of the Southern Pacific Railroad in early September 1876. The S.P. had built south
through the San Joaquin Valley to reach the City of Angels, and while it
worked to span the Tehachapi Mountains and bore the San Fernando
tunnel, crews started grading a roadbed and laying track north out of
Los Angeles to meet the line coming south. The lines met at Lang,

Main Street, Los Angeles, ca. 1875. Just a few blocks from the First Baptist Church of Los Angeles. (History Division, Los Angeles County Museum of Natural History)

California,[5] and that link connected Los Angeles with the routes of the Central Pacific and Union Pacific railroads and opened eastern markets to the "capital" of Southern California. Unfortunately, except for citrus, the national depression kept growth sluggish throughout the remainder of the decade and incidentally kept Winfield Scott on the move.[6]

Scott's success in Los Angeles did not sway the Home Mission Society, and in December 1876 its board once again refused to appoint Scott to Los Angeles, explaining that the appointment would put a strain on the society's coffers. Considering the national depression, that may have been a valid reason. It is also possible that either Scott's close association with Kalloch or his espousal of the social gospel did not set too well with the society's hierarchy. Whatever the reason for the society's reluctance to support Scott, his salary continued to be paid by the Los Angeles church. That December also brought the

Scotts personal joy. Shortly before Christmas, Helen gave birth to their third daughter, Addie W. Scott. Addie had been the name of one of Scott's cousins who died of typhoid fever the previous January, and his newborn daughter most likely received her name in memory of that cousin.

In October 1877 the records of the First Baptist Church of Los Angeles reveal a controversy arising over the length of Scott's service to the congregation, and he resigned within three months. Unfortunately, the records do not reveal the roots of the problem, but perhaps the drought that struck Southern California in 1877 played a role. Its effect on an already poor economic climate proved to be ruinous, and the hard times in Southern California may have caused some of Scott's congregation to chafe under the burden of his salary. It is also possible that some members of the congregation resented the time Scott spent working as secretary of the San Gorgonio Flume Company, a venture the pastor took over early in 1877. For whatever reasons, and for the fifth time in a little over two years, the Scott family packed its belongings and moved on, this time to the little community of Banning, California.

Early in 1877, as the Southern Pacific Railroad extended its tracks east from Indio to the Colorado River near Yuma,* Scott became interested in a venture to build a ten-mile flume out of the mountains near San Gorgonio Pass. Situated about 80 miles east of Los Angeles, the proposed flume would carry firewood down to the railroad tracks to supply the Southern Pacific's woodburning locomotives, which apparently needed the extra fuel to cross the 119 miles of desert between Indio and the river. The original backers of the venture, however, lacked proper financing, and the flume building soon came to a halt.[7] A short time later, Scott made plans to continue the flume and sought the backing of his uncle, George W. Scott. Since coming to California in 1850, George Scott had become a highly successful rancher and farmer, and he agreed to provide the necessary capital to complete the project.

With adequate financing assured, Winfield Scott dispatched Welwood Murray to the San Gorgonio Pass country to secure essential water rights for the flume. Murray bought the necessary water rights from the original backers of the project and, acting as resident manager, soon had workmen cutting sugar pine in the mountains. With roughhewn logs the workmen reconstructed an abandoned mill at the head of Water Canyon and began cutting lumber for the flume. In much the

---

*As the S.P. crews worked north from Los Angeles to meet the line coming south, the railroad also started east toward San Gorgonio Pass and Indio. Regular train service to Indio began in late May, 1876, but further construction ceased until Yuma was designated as the Arizona destination point. [David F. Myrick, *Railroads of Arizona*, vol. 1 (Berkeley: Howell-North Books, 1975), p. 16.]

same fashion that a railroad is built into the wilderness, the flume was built with lumber floated down it to construct each new section. Murray also had a bunkhouse built down in the valley to house the forty men working on the flume and added a store to serve the men and the surrounding ranches and farms. The flume cost $20,000 to complete, and water first flowed to the valley floor on June 3, 1877, less than a month after the railroad reached the Colorado River.

Scott appears to have been on hand for the inauguration of the flume, and later, in July, he took a one-month leave of absence from his Los Angeles church to make a more detailed inspection of his uncle's property. Sometime during his summer visits, Scott preached what was probably the area's first Protestant sermon outdoors under a sycamore tree; the first passenger train rumbled through Banning on September 30, and the Banning Post Office was established October 11. By mid-January Scott had resigned his pastorate and returned with his family to take up residence and run his uncle's company.

When the Scotts arrived to make a new home, Banning had a population of about two hundred people. In addition to the general store, the town included a boardinghouse, four small homes, several tents, two saloons, and no churches. About a month after Scott's arrival, the flume company sold six hundred cords of wood to the Southern Pacific for four dollars a cord, and in March, Banning received its own railroad depot, siding, and station agent. Scott's interest and confidence in the fluming venture brought capital, jobs, and people to the San Gorgonio Pass country, and the completed flume brought recognition from the railroad. The stop for wood also meant a stop to pick up agricultural products, to leave machinery and merchandise, and to pick up and deposit passengers. Although named for Phineas Banning, "the foremost promoter of improved transportation facilities in Southern California,"[8] the community owed its economic genesis to Winfield Scott.

It is doubtful that George W. Scott viewed his nephew's efforts in terms of community building. In a letter he wrote to a brother in 1879, George Scott bemoaned the fluming operation as "a bilk of the first order." He told his brother he had sunk $50,000 into the project, and that it had not been worth ten cents to run. Every month expenses exceeded revenue by several hundred dollars. He called the flume a speculation that Jim's boy, Winfield, had talked him into backing and went on to say that his nephew had "petered out," leaving him to run the flume himself.

Not knowing Scott's reasons for leaving Banning in October 1878, it is difficult to understand why he left his uncle in such a predicament. The only known circumstance that might be offered in explanation was the tragic death of the Scotts' infant daughter in April. In their immediate sorrow, Scott wrote to Isaac Kalloch.

> Our hearts are overwhelmed with grief again in the loss of our little Addie. She died this morning at 7 o'clock after a long illness. We had hopes of her recovery until about three weeks ago, when she was taken with inflammation of the lungs and we could get no relief. She was the pet of our household and sunshine in our home. The good Lord knows why, and we leave all with Him.

Addie was only fifteen months old when she died, and her loss seems to have been especially hard for the Scotts to accept. Her name was never mentioned again in any written recital of Scott family members.

Winfield Scott had begun to homestead when he came to Banning in 1878, taking up a quarter section in the San Gorgonio township. Under the Civil War veterans' amendment to the homestead act, Scott's two-year war service counted toward the five-year occupancy requirement needed to gain patent to the land, and it is reasonable to assume he planned to stay at least three years in order to take title to his 160 acres. Yet within ten months Scott left Banning for San Francisco. In spite of all the counseling of bereaved relatives which Scott must have done in his ministerial career, it is possible that he simply could not handle the death of his infant child and had to get away from the scene of his loss. Of Scott's time in Banning three facts remain. He created the economic base for its early development; personal tragedy befell him there while he worked to develop his homestead and make a paying proposition of his uncle's company; and he abandoned his commitment, leaving his uncle to pick up the pieces of a substantial financial debacle.

George's son Arthur, and Daniel Scott, son of George's brother Gideon, arrived in Banning in September 1878, and it can only be presumed that they came to take over the family business. George Scott bought one thousand acres near the mouth of the flume, and his brother Gideon arrived the following year to farm it for him,[9] presumably making use of the flume as an irrigation canal. With the arrival of his cousins, Winfield Scott returned to San Francisco to become Isaac Kalloch's assistant pastor.

Disappointment, tragedy, and failure punctuated Scott's two years in Southern California, yet during that time he gained a knowledge of irrigated citrus farming which would prove to be invaluable in his later years. While living in Los Angeles and Banning, Scott became familiar with the Riverside colony, a planned agricultural community in which twenty-eight miles of irrigation canals brought water to many thousands of orange trees planted as seedlings in the early 1870s. Situated about fifty miles east of Los Angeles and thirty miles west of Banning,

An 1878 Currier and Ives bird's eye view of San Francisco, looking southwest. Market Street is the wide boulevard running from the bay through the left center portion of the picture. The U.S. Mint with two tall, billowing smokestacks stands on the left-hand side of Market Street where it appears to narrow. Just below the U.S. Mint stands the Metropolitan Temple, crowned by a single cupola. (The Bancroft Library)

The Metropolitan Temple, on the northeast corner of 5th Street and Jessie, just a few yards south of Market Street. In addition to the main auditorium and its $16,000 organ, the Temple featured reading rooms, libraries, gymnasiums, day nurseries, and an additional auditorium on the second floor which seated one thousand. The ground floor's street space was leased to retail establishments with the rents going to the first mortgage holder. (The Bancroft Library)

the Riverside colony, later known simply as Riverside, came into existence as a result of the energetic promotion of Judge John Wesley North. North recruited colonists in the Midwest for his four-thousand-acre community and arranged discount rail fares to entice them west. Unfortunately, many prospective colonists chose the greener coastal areas of California once they arrived, but those who stayed planted orange orchards to provide for their livelihood.

Among those remaining in Riverside was Luther Calvin Tibbetts, who planted two Washington navel orange trees imported from Bahia, Brazil. The Department of Agriculture in Washington, D.C., provided the trees as part of an experiment with seedless navel oranges, hence the name Washington navels, and in 1878 the two trees bore their first fruit. Coupled with the arrival of the Southern Pacific Railroad in Los Angeles eighteen months earlier, this navel orange experiment revolutionized citrus farming in Southern California. The ability to make bulk shipments of oranges to eastern markets with reasonable speed transformed citrus farming over the next ten years from a purely local enterprise to a viable agricultural industry with national markets. The introduction of the Riverside-Washington navel orange in eastern markets and its immediate acceptance there accelerated the transformation. Large demand for the sweet, seedless oranges triggered a frenetic period of planting new orchards and grafting buds from the Tibbetts' trees.[10] Winfield Scott observed the beginning of these developments at close range, and ten years later he used the knowledge gained at Riverside to begin his own citrus experiments, including the planting of Washington navel oranges. In the fall of 1878, however, Scott had to deal with personal loss and personal failure, and his California odyssey continued.

In October 1878 just two years after he left San Francisco, Scott returned there to take up the church's work in the King's Hall Mission. He also began occupying, on a regular basis, Isaac Kalloch's pulpit in the Metropolitan Temple. Completed in 1877, the Metropolitan Temple stood as the largest Baptist church in the United States. The main auditorium accommodated three thousand people with standing room for an additional two thousand. Having made his church the largest in the country, Kalloch delegated his ministerial duties to four assistants and traveled the length of the Pacific Coast "giving lectures, dedicating churches and acting as guest preacher."[11] In addition, Kalloch ventured into the treacherous waters of San Francisco municipal politics.

This was the era in San Francisco's history of Dennis Kearney and his Workingman's party. As times continued hard and jobs scarce for San Francisco's wage earners, they listened intently as Kearney blamed the corporations, the railroads, corrupt politicians, and the Chinese for their problems.[12] Kalloch, at first, denounced the Kearneyites as "the refuse of the Paris Commune. Incendiaries from Berlin and Tipperary. European agitators who are at rest in no country under heaven. The Robespierres of revolution and riot."[13] Against their anti-Chinese position, Kalloch boasted that the Metropolitan Church had "the largest Chinese Sunday School in the world." From the pulpit he declared that he was against the double standard of aiding the Chinese with missions to China while at the same time forbidding them to immigrate to the United States and implied that exclusion was the disreputable half of the proposition.

As economic conditions worsened, Kearney's stock rose, and the Workingman's party gained increasing support. In that changing political climate Kalloch's condemnations slackened and soon ceased. At that same time he also closed his Chinese Sunday school. On the Fourth of July, 1878, Kalloch addressed a large crowd in the Metropolitan Temple. He had been appointed Chaplain of the Day by the city's Fourth of July committee, but instead of speaking to the subject of patriotism, he prayed for the success of the Workingman's cause and reminded the Almighty of their slogans: "Labor Must Be King!", "Have But Honest Men For Officials!", and "The Chinese Must Go!" The followers of Kearney were overjoyed with this conversion to their cause, while Kalloch curbed rising dissent within his congregation by discharging those who spoke out against his political machinations. Such was the situation when Scott returned to San Francisco.

In addition to preaching in the Temple, Scott and his wife conducted the mission school at King's Hall, and Scott edited another small paper, *The Mission Banner*. This busy schedule did not last, however, for the Baptist church in Petaluma, Sonoma County, needed a preacher. During the month of February 1879 Scott commuted to Petaluma as pastoral supply, and in March he received an invitation to become permanent pastor. Kalloch, however, did not want to lose Scott's services. He was busily engaged in writing the Workingman's draft of a new state constitution and needed all the pastoral assistance he could muster, but he reluctantly gave his assistant his blessing to accept the call.

Before leaving for Petaluma, Scott wrote a letter to the editor of the *Standard*, a leading Baptist newspaper published in Chicago. President Rutherford B. Hayes had recently vetoed the first national legislation aimed at restricting Chinese immigration to the United States, and Scott apparently felt that a misunderstanding of the California situation had played a part in the president's veto. Scott tried to explain, as dispassionately as he could, that the California position favoring the exclusion of the Chinese had nothing to do with persecution, as many easterners claimed, but stemmed rather from economic problems created by the presence of large numbers of Chinese in California. Scott asserted that the American workingman was fighting an economic battle for survival and was losing.

> These hordes of aliens move like clouds of locusts in solid phalanx upon all of our industries. They can live on one quarter the amount that a decent white man can. They can eat and thrive on anything from rats to lizards. Having no families, hundreds of them can be packed like sardines in rickety rooms above ground, or cellars below the surface. Competing with them is absolutely out of the question. No white man can do it even were he to remain single.

In Scott's opinion, the only salvation for the American workingman lay in a ban against all Chinese immigration. In defense of this position he asked rhetorically, "Why should America not protect herself? Why should we stretch our liberty to our destruction?" Scott's simplistic and' unconsciously racist point of view typifies the thinking that prevailed in California in the 1870s and represents one of the darkest moments of his career. He failed to look beyond the facade of conventional thinking to see that the hapless Chinese usually took jobs no American would accept. The Chinese had become the scapegoat for the "hard times" in California, and Scott's wholesale acceptance of the anti-Chinese position reflects poorly on his judgment.

Scott's championing of the workingman in California and his acceptance of the conventional answer to their problems is understandable. If for no other reason, his loyalty to Kalloch demanded such a position. However, Scott's statement concerning persecution of the Chinese cannot be understood, for it is totally out of character. In defending the California position Scott flatly stated, "The great mass of all the people are universal in the desire to give them equal protection while here. The cry raised in the East that religious or civic persecution is practiced here is very far from the truth." It is difficult to understand why Scott uttered such a patently untrue statement. For close to thirty years the Chinese in California had been discriminated against, harassed, driven from their homes and businesses, beaten, and sometimes killed, with almost total impunity.[14] Scott was either ignorant of the situation, or, being confronted with massive opposition to a position he supported, he rationalized away reality in order to vindicate himself. He and his friends may have desired to extend the cloak of equal protection to the Chinese, but such cannot be said for the majority of Californians. Scott's sojourn in California continued to be his Achilles' heel.

After serving in Petaluma for less than a year, Scott moved on to aid the Central Baptist Church of Oakland. There in early 1880 the

Scotts' fourth daughter, Florence, was born. Although Scott had served in Oakland just a short while and now had a tiny infant in the family, the Baptist brethren soon called upon him to move once more. In February 1880 he went to San Jose to begin a term as interim pastor in the church he had helped dedicate five years earlier. Sixty new members joined the church during the next four months, but before long, Scott packed his bags once more.[15] It is not clear whether Kalloch prevailed upon Scott to come to his aid or whether Scott came on his own to assist his beleaguered colleague. In any event, the summer found Winfield Scott once again occupying the pulpit of the Metropolitan Temple.

During the period Scott had been away, Kalloch found himself involved in a series of events that read like a dime novel. In June 1879 he became the Workingman's candidate for mayor of San Francisco, and during the heat of the campaign, he entered into a vicious name-calling bout with Charles DeYoung, editor and publisher of the *San Francisco Chronicle*. One Friday, before a crowd of perhaps ten thousand people in front of the Metropolitan Temple, Kalloch responded to an attack on the morality of his father by casting aspersions on DeYoung's mother and calling into question his parentage. When DeYoung heard of Kalloch's remarks, he went to Kalloch's church and shot the preacher at point-blank range, almost killing him. The election had been in some doubt before the shooting, but DeYoung's precipitate action assured Kalloch's victory. Kalloch's new position as mayor did nothing to elevate the enmity between himself and DeYoung, and the newspaper publisher, who had not been charged by the authorities, obtained from Boston a quantity of pamphlets detailing Kalloch's earlier trial for adultery and began to circulate them among prominent businessmen. On April 23, 1880, Isaac M. Kalloch, the minister's son, went to the *Chronicle* office and shot Charles DeYoung to death. Still holding the smoking pistol, the younger Kalloch surrendered to police authorities, who quickly charged him with murder. At about this same time, the elder Kalloch's enemies on the board of supervisors began impeachment proceedings against him on various charges of alleged wrongdoing. Finally, elements within the Baptist State Convention, meeting in mid-May, sought to force Kalloch from the ministry.[16] Beleaguered and besieged on several fronts, Kalloch found less and less time to attend to ministerial duties, and during the summer and fall, Winfield Scott ascended to the pulpit of the Metropolitan Temple on Sunday mornings.

In an incredible trial, Isaac M. Kalloch was acquitted, and his father survived the attempts to strip him of his office and his pulpit. Having helped his colleague in a time of great need, Scott stepped aside

A bird's eye view of Petaluma, 1871. The Baptist church, as indicated by the arrow, is located far from the center of town in the upper left-hand corner of the drawing. Winfield Scott would arrive eight years after this scene was drawn, but the general impression is valid for Scott's time there. (The Bancroft Library)

A bird's eye view of Oakland, as seen from the north. This scene was published in 1881, when the city had a population of thirty-five thousand people. Scott's youngest daughter, Florence, was born here in 1880, while he assisted the Central Baptist Church. (The Bancroft Library)

when Kalloch returned to his congregation. There is no evidence to suggest that Scott played an active role in any of Kalloch's political activities. He remained loyal to his long-time associate and shepherded his congregation. When the maelstrom quieted, Scott moved on to establish a new church in San Francisco, the Jefferson Square Baptist Church. Their home near the church would be the peripatetic Scotts' last in California during their missionary years, and for a time they did not have to live out of their suitcases and trunks. In recognition of Winfield Scott's many contributions to the Baptist cause, both in California and in the rest of the nation, California College awarded him an honorary Doctor of Divinity degree. It was a fitting tribute to five long, unsettled years of dedicated effort in California and to sixteen years of distinguished service to the Baptist cause in the West. The Reverend Mr. Scott became the Reverend Dr. Scott. His journeys, nevertheless, were not over.

CHAPTER VI

Crossroads at Reno

By the spring of 1881, the congregation of the Baptist church of Reno, Nevada, had experienced its fair share of problems. Membership had dwindled from seventy-five to less than fifteen, and the church had been without a pastor for almost a year. Two years previously the house of worship burned to the ground, and even though the congregation began at once to build a new one, by the spring of 1881 all it had to show for its efforts was an uncompleted building, a $2,500 mortgage, and little hope of paying it off. Prospects had appeared brighter the previous summer, when D. Banks McKenzie, a temperance worker, agreed to become their pastor. McKenzie had apparently decided to change careers, and Isaac S. Kalloch, heading a group from his San Francisco church, came to Reno to preside at the ordination service. Unfortunately, it evolved that McKenzie desired the title of reverend only to heighten his prestige in temperance work, and within a few days he abandoned the Reno Baptists and returned to California.[1]

At the request of the Mission Board of the California Baptist Convention, under whose auspices the Reno church resided, Winfield Scott arrived in Reno in mid-May 1881 to spend several weeks helping the struggling congregation find a pastor and begin paying off its debt. As he always did, Scott addressed one of his Sunday services to the young, hoping to get them involved in the church, and, as usual, he achieved immediate success. Not wishing to look further, the members of the church asked Scott to become their pastor. After the evening service on Sunday, May 29, Scott caught the nine o'clock train for California to keep a previous commitment to deliver the Decoration

Day address at San Jose. From there he continued on to San Francisco to once again gather up his family; he had accepted the call of the Reno congregation.

In the spring of 1881, Reno, Nevada, was a town of approximately four thousand people and was served by one bank, two newspapers, three drugstores, four groceries, five churches, six meat markets, seven millinery and dressmaking emporiums, twelve attorneys, and fifteen saloons. Reno had come into being as a result of the construction of the Central Pacific Railroad and served as the forwarding point for goods destined for the mines of Virginia City and the capital at Carson City. Its location in the midst of the fertile Truckee River Valley also made it the center of Nevada's major agricultural region. Over eighty miles of irrigation canals turned the sagebrush covered desert into a verdant oasis. Here would be another important training ground for Winfield Scott in the methods of irrigated farming.

The Reverend Dr. Scott had no small task before him, and he plunged ahead once again with his characteristic energy. On his arrival a choir was organized under the tutelage of a Dr. Springstein and his wife, "both of whom are fine musicians." As has been noted, music played an integral part in the Scott ministry, and good music not only uplifted the spirit but also helped to enlist new members. Just two days after Scott preached his first sermon as their pastor, the members of the congregation welcomed the Scott family with a surprise party at their home. It was a simple way of expressing their appreciation to their new pastor for his commitment to them. The new choir serenaded the gathering, and everyone enjoyed ice cream, cake, and strawberries with cream. It was a happy beginning.

As the weeks and months passed, the church building was finished, the mortgage was reduced, owing in large part to a $1,000 contribution solicited from Kalloch, and the congregation grew.[2] With the success of the choir came encouragement for larger musical undertakings. Professor M. I. Stimson was brought over from San Francisco to conduct singing classes for the church and its friends. As these classes enjoyed a growing popularity, the interest in choral music spread beyond the confines of the Baptist church. In late April 1882 a music convention was hosted by Scott's congregation, with delegates attending from all over western Nevada. Organized by Professor Stimson and supported by Pastor Scott, the convention provided the "best musical entertainment ever given in the state." Public concerts were supplemented by workshops in which delegates were instructed in the finer points of choral music. Apparently Scott's speaking voice was also suited to singing, and he participated in the convention by singing in a quartet with three women from the community. Wherever Scott

Virginia Street, Reno, Nevada, 1882. (Nevada State Historical Society)

went, he became more to the community than just the Baptist preacher. Reno proved no exception.

The Home Mission Society of New York once again lent its support to Scott, providing $300 of his $1,200 salary. Although prices had followed a steep downward trend between 1865 and 1879 and although wages had shown a slight decline following the Panic of 1873,[3] this one-third reduction in salary from what Scott purportedly received in Los Angeles must have given him pause for reflection. Having to rely from year to year on the vote of boards and committees to determine one's income did not augur well for a comfortable future, and having to pull up roots continually was not especially conducive to family life either. Although he served his church without hesitation, the constant shifting about of recent years would have taxed the goodwill of any man. When Scott returned to gather his family for the trip to Reno in early June 1881, he made the decision to try to create a more viable future for himself. On June 4, 1881, he made application to the Secretary of War, Robert T. Lincoln, to become a chaplain in the United States Army.

The position of army chaplain was a coveted appointment among the clergy who sought it. It was a secure government post which paid $2,200 per year. Moreover, it was difficult to obtain, as there were but thirty-four positions in the entire army and only as many openings as death, resignation, or retirement capriciously provided. One needed more than good personal credentials to secure an appointment, and Scott called upon all the goodwill at his disposal to gain his place in the system. As he had crossed the country in his mission work, Scott had made many friends. A surprising number of them possessed considerable political influence, and at his request, they came to his aid. United States Senator John F. Miller, Republican from California, sponsored Scott's application. In approaching Miller, Scott was quite candid.

> I will esteem it a personal and great favor if you will present the application and assist me with your influence to secure it.
>
> I have fought a hard and I trust not unsuccessful battle in my ministerial work since the War, and now if I could secure this position it would help greatly to make the balance of my days comfortable for myself and my family.
>
> I know an old Comrade will appreciate the statement that other things being equal, an old soldier with an unsullied record should be entitled to these positions.
>
> I have always been true to the old flag, and have stood squarely and fearlessly with the Republican party since its organization until the present time.*

---

*Winfield Scott rarely wrote the word *and* in his correspondence, preferring instead to use a figure similar to the symbol "+." Most of the *ands* used in direct quotation from his correspondence are substitutions for his symbol, but instead of bracketing each one to indicate this substitution, the practice is noted here.

Scott ended this letter in a manner that indicated he clearly understood political patronage. He closed saying, " . . . believing that I will be able to prove myself worthy of this position if I receive it and capable of appreciating the favors of my friends, and reciprocating in every way in my power." Miller found the argument persuasive and joined in the effort.

United States Senator John P. Jones, Republican from Nevada, seconded Miller's efforts and worked behind the scenes to line up Senate support for Scott. United States Senators George M. Chilcott and Nathaniel P. Hill, Republicans from Colorado, Elbridge G. Lapham, Republican from New York, and John J. Ingalls, Republican from Kansas, also wrote letters of recommendation. Perhaps of even greater significance were the recommendations of United States Senators Francis M. Cockrell, Democrat from Missouri, and James G. Fair, Democrat from Nevada. These men had nothing to gain politically from recommending staunch Republican Scott to this position. This is especially true of Cockrell who was a former Confederate officer and came from a state where Scott had little if any following. These recommendations could not be considered politically motivated.

Republican congressman from Rochester, New York, John Van Voorhis added his words of praise to those of the senators, but again, perhaps the more significant praise came from Democratic congressman from Nevada, George W. Cassidy. Cassidy was an old-line Democrat and a newspaperman who published the Eureka *Sentinel*. Of Scott, Cassidy enthused, "He is a gentleman of great moral worth and character, and that for these and other qualities of heart and mind, he is universally esteemed where ever [*sic*] known throughout the West." Nathan Cole, former Republican mayor of St. Louis and former congressman from Missouri, and also a cousin of Scott's father, supported Scott's application and worked to gain the support of others for his friend. Said Cole to Secretary Lincoln, "I do desire to commend M. Scott as one not only worthy, but as deserving, if anyone might be thus mentioned, of your kind and favorable consideration . . . . He is a grand and noble man." Finally, in an extraordinary gesture, the officers of the state of Nevada, including the governor, the attorney general, the secretary of state, and the chief justice of the state supreme court, signed a letter endorsing Scott's application. Taken in sum, it was a remarkable outpouring of goodwill from a powerful group of friends and acquaintances.

In addition to the politicians, Scott received endorsements from nonpolitical friends and colleagues as well. Officers and men of the 126th New York Volunteers and friends in and around Geneva, New York, forty-seven in all, signed a petition on their comrade's behalf.

The members of his District War Committee, including the then current secretary of the treasury, Charles J. Folger, wrote a letter of recommendation for Scott. Professor David H. Robinson of the University of Kansas wrote a letter for his old classmate which included the signature of the dean of the Education Department and professor of natural history, Frank H. Snow. Snow knew Scott from his Leavenworth days when the professor helped the young preacher with his lecture series. The president of the University of Rochester, Martin B. Anderson, also put his prestige behind Scott's application, noting that he "has done excellent pioneer work in our Western States and Territories." The G.A.R. posts in Nevada and California to which Scott belonged sent along their strongest recommendations. Some recommendations were made out of political expediency or for political gain, some were perfunctory, but the majority were genuine and enthusiastic. They are yet another gauge of Winfield Scott the man. Unfortunately for Scott, there were no vacancies immediately available, and his application was put on file. He would be in Reno longer than he hoped.

Scott did not give up his efforts to become a chaplain and continued to solicit endorsements. He also worked to erase the debt of the Reno church and to bring music to the people of Reno. During this period another anti-Chinese campaign was being waged on the Pacific Coast. Congress was being pressed once more to pass a Chinese Exclusion Act. The previous bill to prohibit Chinese immigration had been vetoed by the president, and a renewed effort was being pressed to force the issue upon him again. Scott continued to favor the prohibition of Chinese immigration, and he peppered the eastern press with strongly felt letters on the subject. His letters to the editor aroused a great deal of comment in the East, and he was invited to visit the East Coast to debate the Chinese question. Immediately following the Reno music convention, Scott took a two-month leave of absence and journeyed east. He had kept ties with his friends, colleagues, and congregations as he had moved west, and on this journey east, he renewed those ties by stopping off in Denver and Leavenworth to preach in the churches he had built.

In the meantime, letters continued to arrive in Washington supporting his application. When a vacancy finally developed, President Chester A. Arthur sent Scott's name to the Senate for confirmation. It is interesting that President Arthur, who vetoed the Chinese Exclusion Bill, would grant an appointment to such a vocal opponent of Chinese immigration. Scott's reputation apparently transcended this issue. He was confirmed by the Senate July 27, 1882. The Reverend Dr. Winfield Scott was about to embark on a new career.

Scott received orders to report to Vancouver Barracks, head-quarters of the Department of the Columbia, for assignment by the commanding officer, Brigadier General Nelson A. Miles. The chaplain had hoped to be assigned to Fort Leavenworth. A Rochester classmate was commanding officer there, many old friends resided in the area, and there were excellent educational opportunities for his two younger daughters. Fort Leavenworth, however, had been promised to another chaplain. Mistakenly believing he was to be assigned to Vancouver Barracks instead, Scott wrote that this would be a satisfactory appointment with regard to the education of his girls. But this station was not to be his either. Scott was assigned to Fort Coeur D'Alene, Idaho Territory. Until quarters could be prepared for him at Fort Coeur D'Alene, the chaplain received a temporary posting to Fort Canby, Washington Territory. Fort Canby was a lonely outpost, situated appropriately on Cape Disappointment, which guarded the mouth of the Columbia River. There on October 11, 1882, Winfield Scott reported for duty.

CHAPTER VII

The Chaplain Years

To reach Fort Canby from the sea, it was necessary to navigate the treacherous passage through the mouth of the Columbia River into Baker Bay. A sandbar, pounded by the surf, nearly blocked the mouth of the river, and the narrow channel through to the bay could be safely negotiated only at high tide and in good weather. Many a captain unfamiliar with the passage had gone aground in his attempt to get through. Arriving by steamer from San Francisco, Winfield Scott learned of these hazards at the same time that he learned they had missed the tide by forty-five minutes. It was then nine in the morning, and they would have to stand offshore until three in the afternoon when the tide came in again. Having been unable to keep anything in his stomach for more than two days, Scott's distress at this turn of events is not difficult to imagine, but whatever his feelings that morning, it is doubtful that they compared with what he felt that afternoon. Just twenty minutes before three, a thick fog enveloped the ship, and another eighteen hours of tossing at anchor awaited the suffering chaplain. Winfield Scott did not soon forget the sandbar at the mouth of the Columbia.

Fort Canby was a heavy artillery post built during the Civil War to help protect the Union's far western boundaries.[1] When Scott arrived, the garrison consisted of thirty enlisted men and three officers of the Twenty-first Infantry, a lifeboat crew of seven, a lighthouse crew of four, and the families of some of the men. Accustomed to small flocks, the chaplain set about his official duties with dispatch.

There being no suitable place to hold worship services on the post, a room above the guardhouse was secured for God's work and fitted

with rough-hewn benches. Whether from a different religious preference or a total lack of same, Scott found few soldiers inclined to attend
his Sunday services and sought other means to improve the moral tone
of the post. He decided to give lectures on historic, literary, and moral
subjects during the week, hoping to stimulate an interest in reading,
which, to Scott's manner of thinking, would create a climate of interest
in his religious services. Always a believer in music, he coupled his
lectures with group singing, and from his monthly reports to the adjutant general of the United States, it is learned his efforts proved successful. Attendance began to increase at Sunday services.

In the interim, while he attempted to nurture an interest in things
religious, he reduced his Sunday services at the post to one every other
week and broadened the scope of his ministry to include the surrounding countryside. He held services at Ilwaco, a small fishing village two miles from Canby on Baker Bay. Every other Sunday he held
morning services there, returning to the post for services at three in the
afternoon. On the alternate Sundays, he journeyed fourteen miles
across and up the river to the prosperous community of Astoria, Oregon. There he organized a Sunday school and held three services on the
Sabbath. Scott's missionary instincts remained strong.

In addition to Sunday services at the post, Scott's duties included
calling on the families on the post, visiting the sick, and consoling the
miscreants in the guardhouse. When asked, he also attended to the
marriages and funerals of the civilian population in the neighborhood
and, as an additional responsibility, served with the lifeboat crew,
which was often called upon to rescue imprudent sailors from the
sandbar across the mouth of the Columbia River. In later years he
would recall that after several dunkings while on lifeboat duty, and with
the frequent rain, he finally realized why the powers that be had sent a
Baptist to Fort Canby.

The services in Ilwaco and Astoria became increasingly popular,
and Scott was constantly on the move. In late January 1883 he held
services in Ilwaco every night. In February he baptized nine persons in
Astoria, and by late May he had enrolled seventy-five "scholars" in
Sunday school there. On one particular Sunday, sandwiched between
the morning service in Ilwaco and the afternoon service at the post,
Scott conducted a service at the head of Shoal Water Bay, nine miles
from Canby. The man's energy seemed boundless.

After a year's work at Fort Canby, Chaplain Scott received a
transfer across the river to Fort Stevens, Oregon. Fort Stevens had
been constructed during the Civil War to serve as sentry on the opposite side of the Columbia River from Fort Canby. As a temporary
posting within a temporary posting, Scott's transfer came at a time

Fort Canby, Washington, 1890. Photograph was taken from the slope of Cape Disappointment. Note the guard house standing on pilings in the left middle ground on the shore of Baker Bay. (Oregon Historical Society)

Guard house at Fort Canby. Second story served as the post chapel during Chaplain Scott's tenure there. (Quartermaster General Photograph, National Archives)

when the Twenty-first Infantry detachment stationed at Canby was replaced by two batteries of the First Artillery. It seems clear from correspondence that the new commanding officer of the fort, a Captain James MacMurray, had little use for Chaplain Scott. MacMurray wrote that most of his men were either of the Roman Catholic or Episcopal persuasion. He did not state that Scott was neither needed nor wanted, but the implication is clear. Scott's new flock at Fort Stevens consisted of ten men, but the opportunity to continue working in the surrounding communities compensated for the lack of military parishioners.

In December 1883 Scott received a seventeen-day leave of absence to conduct religious services in Seattle. The first city of Washington Territory boasted a population of over thirty-five hundred, had recently secured rail connections, and was building the first street railway in the territory.[2] As a result of Scott's prodigious efforts in Seattle, the Baptist church was richer by fifty members. The sojourn also prompted him to write the adjutant general of the United States concerning the work of army chaplains on the frontier. Scott held the view that the work the chaplains did in the small communities adjacent to frontier posts should not be "charged against them as leaves of absence." He thought the chaplains performed a service to their country by caring for the religious needs of the civilian population which, on the frontier, was often bereft of moral sustenance. Therefore, he argued, chaplains should not be penalized for this professional work. He closed by saying,

> If department commanders could be permitted to allow chaplains to do such work a closer bond of sympathy would be established between the army and the people at these frontier posts, while the chaplains who had the strength and dispositions to do this extra work would be a force for good in all these frontier settlements.
>
> The chaplain who was warmed into spiritual life and activity by this contact with the people, would be less liable to be lifeless and perfunctory in the discharge of his post duties.

General Miles, commander of the department, agreed with Scott and endorsed the proposal when he forwarded the chaplain's monthly report to Washington. The secretary of war, however, was not inclined to tamper with army regulations, and the matter ended. Chaplain Scott, nevertheless, continued ministering to the civilian population with the time logged against him, although, as Captain MacMurray hastened to point out, Scott did receive compensation from the civilians to whom he preached. His activities away from the post, therefore, should not be considered acts of altruism. Scott was an enthusiastic and energetic preacher whose basic goal in life was to serve, but he also hoped to provide a secure future for his family, and he worked hard toward that end.

For a time in January 1884 a small detachment of the Twenty-first Infantry from Vancouver Barracks swelled the chaplain's flock. Other detachments came and went with garrison life remaining thoroughly routine except for their arrivals and departures. By late 1884 there were so few men at Stevens that Scott conducted his work on a one-to-one basis, with most of his energies directed toward his congregation in Astoria.

Astoria in 1884 was a thriving community of five thousand inhabitants. It relied heavily on salmon fishing and the canning industry, which gave it a sufficient economic base to acquire the amenities of electricity, water, and gas. One of the major canning companies was Kinney Brothers, and the Kinneys belonged to the Baptist church. In years past their contributions to the church had made possible the acquisition of property and the construction of a house of worship, and Scott undoubtedly called upon them to provide for the new coat of paint applied to the inside of the church and for the baptistry that was constructed to receive his new converts. Although he was a chaplain in the United States Army, he endeavored to help the church prosper as if it were his own. If the army chose not to utilize his time and experience, there were others who would, and although his contributions may seem inconsequential in the broader context of history, his service to his fellowman was outstanding in any context.

In August 1884 Scott's temporary postings appeared to be coming to an end. *The Astorian* reported that his many friends would be happy to know that he would be among them for a while longer, but that he would probably be transferred to Angel Island in San Francisco Bay after the first of the year. In the meantime, garrison life continued as usual, and in October a detachment of the Fourteenth Infantry reported to Stevens on an engineering assignment. In chronicling their stay at the fort, Scott's temperance colors were revealed. "The morals have been excellent. Not a man has been under the influence of liquor during the month." The adjutant general would hear more on this subject in the years to come, for Chaplain Scott was an inveterate opponent of "demon rum." During December 1884 all troops were withdrawn from Fort Stevens, leaving Scott alone to tend to his church in Astoria. His temporary duty was coming to an end. Orders finally came through in February 1885 assigning him to Angel Island where he reported March 6, 1885.

The military installation on Angel Island had been constructed during the Civil War for many of the same reasons that had occasioned the construction of Forts Canby and Stevens. Situated in a beautiful natural setting, the post at the time of Scott's arrival was home for the Eighth Infantry, commanded by Colonel August V. Kautz. The colonel's wife was a vivacious hostess whose receptions and dances, requiring full-dress uniform, added color and life to the post. Although it would prove to be a decidedly mixed blessing for Mrs. Scott, the chaplain's appointment there must have come as a welcome change for them. San Francisco was only forty-five minutes away by the government steamboat which made the circuit of the military posts of San Francisco Bay.[3] In the city, and in Oakland, old friendships and acquaintances were renewed. The Scotts' new home commanded the most magnificent view from anywhere on the island. Situated on the slope of the hill between the chapel and the parade ground, the house looked out upon an expanse of emerald green lawn and across the blue green waters of the bay to the Golden Gate. A more agreeable setting in which to pursue God's work is hard to imagine.

Scott lost no time in beginning his duties. Within ten days of his arrival he had organized a Sunday school and was conducting three services each Sabbath. He once again held services away from the post and gave lectures both on the post and in San Francisco, in addition to his visitations to the prisoners in the guardhouse, to the sick in the post

Fort Stevens, Oregon, 1906. View of the post taken from a water tower toward the Columbia River seen in the background. Fort Stevens received modifications and improvements after Scott's duty there, but the general outlines of the installation remained the same. Note the heavy gun emplacements to the left of the post buildings down toward the river. (Oregon Historical Society)

Astoria, Oregon, ca. 1881. The large stone building in the center foreground is the customs house. Note also the plank sidewalks and partially planked streets. (Oregon Historical Society)

hospital, and to the families of the soldiers. One final duty involved superintending the post school and its one teacher.

Winfield Scott served on Angel Island for four years, and it seems to have been a particularly hard time for Helen Scott. As the chaplain's wife, she constantly entertained both military and civilian guests. In addition, her three daughters, ages five to twenty, called on her time and emotions. The eldest, Minnie, left home during this period to pursue a career in education, while Helen, aged seventeen, met an Oakland lad and soon became the first daughter to be married. Florence, the youngest, required the attention any five-year-old would need. Unaccustomed to such a hectic pace and to such a worldly atmosphere, and apparently not endowed with her husband's stamina or enthusiasm, Helen Scott suffered frequent headaches, loss of weight, and fatigue.

There were good moments as well, and the marriage of her daughter Helen to Edward Dubois Flint of Oakland was certainly one. Spring had arrived in California, and the Scotts' small home was festooned with a profusion of flowers of every description. Outside in the garden, adding pomp and color in their full-dress uniforms with white-plumed helmets, the band of the First Infantry serenaded the arriving guests. An extra boat was put into service to ferry all the guests from San Francisco. Major General Oliver O. Howard, commanding general of the Department of California, and his family were taken aboard at the Presidio along with other officers and their wives. Scott's Uncle George, Aunt Amaretta, and brother George were also in attendance for the ceremony. With the band playing Mendelsohn's wedding march, the bride and groom joined the chaplain in the library, and there, with a trembling voice revealing his emotions, he united them in marriage. It was an impressive ceremony in a beautiful setting with a sparkling array of guests. After so many years of enduring the privations of the frontier, it must surely have gladdened Helen Scott's heart to have their daughter married in such a grand and elegant manner.

The four years on Angel Island were busy ones for Chaplain Scott. He usually conducted two sets of services every Sunday, two at the post and two elsewhere. During the summer of 1886, with Angel Island quiet during the changing of regiments, he was assigned to temporary duty at the Presidio, the military installation that covers the northern tip of the San Francisco peninsula. In early 1887, with Scott now shepherding the First Infantry, two of his favorite avocations surfaced when he organized the Army Literary and Temperance Organization of Angel Island. The group had an initial membership of nineteen, which somewhat belies the stereotype of the frontier soldier. General Howard

Partial view of the barracks and parade ground, Angel Island, looking toward San Francisco Bay. (Quartermaster General Photograph, National Archives)

View of the military installation on Angel Island. The chapel, with white spire, can be seen on the hill behind the post. (Quartermaster General Photograph, National Archives)

lent his considerable influence to the undertaking by presenting an early lecture on the Battle of Gettysburg. During the summer of 1887 the First Infantry went into summer camp at Santa Cruz, California, with eight companies billeted within the town of seven thousand. Every Sunday afternoon for two months Scott conducted services for the regiment in an outdoor pavilion. The townspeople were invited to attend, and between eight hundred and one thousand persons crowded the enclosure. These bountiful numbers must have heartened the old campaigner, taking him back to his term of service at the Metropolitan Temple and to the "Baptist Tabernacle" on the plains of Kansas. Scott's effectiveness that summer may be gauged by an invitation he received the following autumn to dedicate a church in Santa Cruz. He took an eleven-day leave of absence in November, and while in Santa Cruz, he conducted eight services for his new friends. At about this time Scott received another invitation that would have a momentous impact on his life and the lives of many others. He was invited to visit the Salt River Valley of Arizona.

CHAPTER VIII

Salt River Valley Farm

In mid-February 1888 "full of doubts . . . skepticism and prejudice," Winfield Scott journeyed to Phoenix, Arizona, on a short leave of absence from his Angel Island post. He had received an invitation to visit the Salt River Valley from a group of civic and business leaders who wanted to promote Phoenix and the surrounding country. They had heard of Scott's reputation as an effective promoter of immigration, most likely through his friend, Robert W. Pearson, pastor of the Phoenix Episcopal Church, and they hoped to enlist Scott's aid in their promotional efforts. These Phoenix men reasoned that once Scott saw the Salt River Valley, he would be won over by its natural advantages and would be willing to help promote its potential. They were correct. After touring the valley for only a week, he became a believer.

Scott used Phoenix as his base of operations, and he described the desert community as "a city of 5,000 or 6,000 inhabitants that has not outgrown the country. It has good schools and hotels and all denominations are represented by churches and edifices either built or being built." A likely source for Scott's population figure was the business community, especially since A. Leonard Meyer's 1888 business directory claimed 5,000 residents for Phoenix, but that estimate can be considered accurate only if winter visitors are included in the total. The historian Hubert Howe Bancroft probably came closer to a correct figure when he wrote that Phoenix "is a thriving town of some 3,000 inhabitants." Bancroft went on to describe Phoenix as being "built largely of adobe, but with many structures of brick and wood . . . [and] now distinguished among Arizona towns for its wealth of shade trees and attractive homes."[1]

It is debatable whether adobe predominated over brick and wood at this time, but the many substantial business buildings in the central downtown area gave adequate testimony to the improving fortunes of the desert community. A branch line of the Southern Pacific Railroad had reached Phoenix from the south in 1887, giving the town its first rail connection,[2] and in addition to its schools, churches, and fine homes, Phoenix was lighted by gas, traversed by a mule-drawn streetcar, and served by seven hotels and boardinghouses, eight restaurants, and two oyster saloons. Ten Chinese laundries, two ice plants, one brewery, five interpreters in Maricopa and Pima Indian, Chinese, Spanish, French, and Italian, and nineteen retail liquor dealers also catered to the wants of the citizenry. Eighteen attorneys and twenty real estate dealers made their homes and livelihoods in the community, and this fact alone may give some indication of why Scott had been invited to help promote Phoenix.

With a farmer's practiced eye, Scott rode about the valley marveling at its productivity and its potential. Grains and forage crops grew abundantly, and after riding for eighteen miles past fields of alfalfa, varying from one to two miles in width, Scott commented that in California a field of ten to twenty acres was considered a fortune. He also expressed surprise at the good condition of the orchards and vineyards and noted the absence of citrus. Citrus farming had yet to be introduced to this desert valley, and Scott, having witnessed firsthand the cultivation of irrigated citrus orchards in the Riverside area of Southern California, recognized the citrus potential of the Salt River Valley. With its extensive irrigation system, dry climate, and fertile soil, the Salt River Valley was as well suited as any area of Southern California for the raising of citrus, and Scott offered this opinion in a speech to Phoenix businessmen at Patton's Opera House.

In his talk to the Salt River Valley's business community, Scott offered advice on the promotion of immigration to their area and recalled the successes of the Kansas immigration effort. He spoke of the current lines of migration west of the Mississippi River, concluded that the Southwest had become the "special focal point" of that migration, and added that judging from his brief stay, Phoenix had a winter climate superior to any he had encountered on the Pacific Coast. Scott made favorable comparisons between the Salt River Valley and other parts of the country, and although it is not recorded whether he made a firm commitment to his hosts to promote their valley, it is clear he had become an immediate convert to their cause.

Returning to Angel Island, Scott resumed his duties, and during March and April he held Sunday services at both his post and Fort Mason, a sixty-eight-acre installation located on Point San Jose, south of the Presidio,[3] on San Francisco Bay. In late May Scott requested another leave of absence, this time for six months to visit his elderly parents whom he had not seen in six years. He clearly implied that he wanted one last chance to visit them before they passed away, but in closing his letter, Scott revealed what was probably the primary purpose of the requested leave and what probably had prompted the earlier Phoenix invitation. He wrote, almost as an afterthought, "I have, also, important business to attend to, which will command the most of my attention for this length of time." The "important business" involved an exposition of Pacific Coast products to be held in Columbus, Ohio, in September. Chaplain Scott had charge of the entire exposition.

Scott was a member of the joint committee of the California Board of Trade and the California Department of the G.A.R. which was arranging for an exhibit of California products and resources to be shown at the annual encampment of the G.A.R. in Columbus, Ohio. The encampment of this Civil War veterans' organization was being held in conjunction with the celebration of the Ohio Centennial and was scheduled to begin September 12. Chaplain Scott received a five-month leave of absence and left Angel Island June 15 to begin preparations for the grand exposition of Pacific Coast products. Nevada and Oregon had joined California in preparing for this exposition, and Scott extended an invitation to Arizona to join its Pacific neighbors. At his suggestion, the California Board of Trade offered Arizona free and ample exhibit space in the exposition hall, and it only remained for the people of Phoenix to grasp the opportunity.

All Phoenicians were invited by the Immigration Union of Maricopa County to an open meeting the evening of June 22, on the plaza in front of the new city hall. N. A. Morford, publisher of the *Phoenix Herald* and vice-president of the Immigration Union, chaired the gathering and introduced Chaplain Scott, who lived up to his reputation as an interesting and persuasive speaker. He spoke with enthusiasm and conviction concerning the merits of the Salt River Valley, and he earnestly advocated the grand exposition as an effective means of advertising the advantages of the valley. Scott's remarks kindled a lively enthusiasm, fanned by the speakers who followed. Leading Phoenicians such as Albert C. Baker, John Y. T. Smith, and William J. Murphy spoke in favor of accepting California's invitation and of joining forces with the communities south of the Salt River in preparing Arizona's exhibit. When W. J. Murphy made a motion that a vote of thanks be extended "to Chaplain Scott and to the California Board of Trade for their generous offers and kind assistance, it was unanimously adopted with rousing cheers."

The next evening some 150 Phoenicians met at the Maricopa and

C. J. Dyer's bird's eye view of Phoenix, 1890. Note Camelback Mountain in the upper right-hand corner of the drawing and the territorial asylum in the far right middle ground. The legend for this thirty-by-forty-inch drawing credits Phoenix with a population of seven thousand people. The buildings which are individually pictured are identified as follows: Bottom Row (l. to r.) Residence of M. H. Sherman, Residence of Clark Churchill, County Courthouse, City Hall, Vendome House, Residence of Ben Butler; Top Row (l. to r.) Daily *Gazette* Office, Monihan Building, Porter Building, Commercial Hotel, Hartford Bank Building, Daily *Herald* Office. (Arizona Department of Library, Archives and Public Records)

NIX
ONA
ER VALLEY
NORTHEAST

REFERENCES

COMMERCIAL HOTEL

HATFORD MARINE CO BUILDING

DALY HERALD OFFICE

CITY HALL

VENDOME HOUSE

RES. OF BEN BUTLER

PHOENIX ARIZONA.

COPYRIGHT 1890 BY C. J. DYER.

Phoenix Railroad depot for a train ride to Tempe. The "north side" of the river planned to extend the hand of cooperation to the "south side." The train was met by Tempe dignitaries Charles Trumbull Hayden, William J. Kingsbury, and Hiram B. Farmer, principal of the Normal School. The Phoenix brass band led the procession to the center of the Tempe business district where rows of benches had been set up in front of the Davis Hotel. W. J. Kingsbury was nominated and elected chairman of the meeting and after a few brief remarks, introduced Scott whose stirring words once again evoked "visible and audible enthusiasm." His remarks were seconded by men from both sides of the river, and a committee was appointed from Tempe, Mesa, and Lehi to meet with one from Phoenix to set up an exhibit of Salt River Valley products Phoenix brass band led the procession to the center of the Tempe business district where rows of benches had been set up in front of the Davis Hotel. W. J. Kingsbury was nominated Salt River Valley Exhibition Association. Said the *Herald*, "The move is one that should have been put on foot long ago." The needed catalyst came in the form of a Baptist preacher who had more vision than most men, and the energy and conviction to make that vision a reality.

Before leaving Phoenix in late June for the reunion of Civil War veterans at Gettysburg, Scott made arrangements to transform his enthusiasm into action. He decided to purchase, under the provisions of the Desert Land Act of March 3, 1877, a section of land about ten miles northeast of Phoenix. On July 2, 1888, at the United States land office in Tucson, an unknown agent for Scott made a down payment of fifty cents per acre on Section 23, Township 2 North, Range 4 East, Gila and Salt River Meridian. The genesis of Scottsdale, Arizona, is found here. Today, bounded by Scottsdale Road on the west, Indian School Road on the south, Hayden Road on the east, and Chaparral Road on the north, Scott's desert land claim lies in the heart of Scottsdale.

Before Scott, other men had made down payments on all or part of Section 23. Morris Goldwater, the prominent Prescott merchant, made a Desert Land Entry on all of Section 23 on April 2, 1885. The Arizona Canal, which crossed the northwest corner of Section 23, was practically finished, and land along its length could soon be irrigated and farmed. Goldwater's entry was canceled, however, on September 12, 1885. Three weeks later, Henry A. Woods of Detroit, Michigan, filed on 520 acres of Section 23. Woods had been general superintendent of the first company to attempt to dig the Panama Canal, but he was in Arizona in search of land investments. In addition to the acreage in Section 23, Woods purchased other property in the valley, but on June 28, 1888, for reasons unknown, he relinquished claim to the 520 acres of

Section 23. Four days later Scott's claim was filed, and the course of development of that small piece of Arizona desert was set in motion. It must be added, however, to put Scott's position in proper perspective, that if it had not been for W. J. Murphy and his successful efforts to build the Arizona Canal, there would have been no immediate, compelling reason to purchase Section 23 under the Desert Land Act. As is ever the case when dealing with the history of the Salt River Valley, water is the key. W. J. Murphy provided this key, and Winfield Scott used it to unlock the productivity of his part of the Arizona desert.

There were other landowners in the immediate vicinity of Section 23 whose land purchases predated Scott's.* They, too, had filed under the Desert Land Act of 1877, which required that land claimed under the act be irrigated within three years. These landowners had complied with this provision but had gone no further. They were not farmers; they were speculators, interested only in the rise in land values. In this regard they were not unique. By 1887 over half of those who had filed desert land claims in Arizona lived in Chicago, St. Louis, Detroit, or some similar eastern location and had little, if any, intention of farming in Arizona. Similarly, less than 15 percent of those filing desert land claims in Arizona between the inception of the act and 1891 ever took title to their land.[4] Winfield Scott proved to be the exception, and it remained for him to begin the civilizing process, to initiate farming, to plant vineyards and orchards, to make a home in the desert. In July 1888, however, groundbreaking on Scott's section of land was still six months away, and he had other commitments to meet.

When Scott left Phoenix in late June, he was embarking upon an extended eastern journey during which he would be called upon to play many roles. His first stop was Gettysburg where he took part in the G.A.R. reunion commemorating the momentous battle fought there. In this instance, his roles were those of participant and official representative, for he was both a veteran of the Battle of Gettysburg and the department chaplain of the California G.A.R. After the Gettysburg reunion, he journeyed to Lancaster, Pennsylvania, at the invitation of Charles W. Mills. Mills had been a fruit dealer in Lancaster for many years, but now he was an enthusiastic Phoenix booster and had returned to Lancaster to organize a colony of Pennsylvanians to migrate to his adopted home. Mills needed the chaplain's infectious enthusiasm

---

Ephraim J. Bennitt, cashier of the Valley Bank, filed on Section 13, directly northeast of Scott's Section 23, on March 25, 1885. On that same date, Hattie E. Sherman, wife of Moses H. Sherman, president of the Phoenix Street Railway Company, filed on Section 25, directly southeast of Section 23. Nannie C. Utley, niece of W. J. Murphy, filed on Section 26, directly south of Section 23, on September 15, 1886. Samuel A. Murphy, brother of W. J. Murphy, filed on 480 acres of Section 27, directly southwest of Section 23, on May 6, 1885. Finally, Albert G. Utley, Nannie's uncle, filed on Section 35, directly south of his niece's Section 26, on June 5, 1886.

to help stimulate the project, and Scott willingly obliged. While visiting Mills, Scott also spoke to audiences in other small towns in Lancaster County. In these instances his role was that of promoter of immigration, and he was well received wherever he went.

Scott was a one-man chamber of commerce for both Arizona and California, but his emphasis now seemed to center on the Salt River Valley. He described this valley as the largest irrigable land area in the West and compared its fertility to that of the valley of the Nile. The climate of the Salt River Valley, Scott avowed, was perfect for the raising of fruit, especially raisins, at that time the most profitable of all fruit industries. In addition, he noted that Phoenix held a slight advantage over California, because her fruit ripened a month earlier and was two days closer to eastern markets. The vivid picture Scott painted made the Salt River Valley come alive to the farmers of the East. Scott was tireless in his travels and lecturing, and the *Phoenix Herald* approvingly recorded his successes.

In September Scott assumed the role of superintendent of the Pacific Coast exhibition at the annual G.A.R. encampment and the Ohio Centennial. In terms of exposure the exposition was a great success, for it was estimated that approximately seventy-five thousand veterans and three hundred thousand visitors came to Columbus to participate in the festivities and to view the exhibits.* On the final day of the encampment, the California delegation passed out hundreds of baskets of fresh fruit. Grapes, peaches, pears, and other fruit from the "Golden State" seconded Scott's lecture tour most tellingly. What an impressive way to advertise a state's horticultural resources! Although it is not known whether the baskets were distributed at Scott's instruction, the gesture certainly evidenced his thinking and most certainly had his blessing.

With the encampment adjourned, Scott remained in the Midwest and East visiting old friends and relatives. In major cities and small towns, he continued to lecture on California and the Salt River Valley. Staying in Indianapolis with an old school friend from Farmer Village, Scott not only lectured on Arizona but supplied the pulpit of the Baptist church for a month while the pastor was on vacation. From Indianapolis he made a quick trip to Chicago to lecture on Arizona and to visit with his sister Minnie. All the visiting and lecturing required more time than expected, and in mid-October Scott asked for, and received, an additional month's leave. On his return trip to California, he stopped in Phoenix, where he made his desert land purchase known to the

---

*The Salt River Valley Exhibition Association, by this time renamed the Maricopa Exhibit Association, was unable to assemble an exhibit in time for the Ohio Centennial, but it did participate that summer in the shipment of the first carload of fresh fruit from the Salt River Valley.

George Washington Scott, Winfield Scott's youngest brother and Scottsdale's first citizen in residence. (Mrs. Lena Scott Polglase, Santa Cruz, California)

Phoenix Herald and indicated that his brother George Washington Scott would soon arrive from San Francisco to begin the work of clearing, ditching, and planting. He then hurried on to Angel Island and a resumption of his ministerial duties.

It is probable that Scott now asked for a transfer to Fort Huachuca, Arizona Territory, in order to be nearer his nascent fruit ranch. There is no record of such a request in his army personnel file, but in February 1889 a transfer was ordered. On his journey to Fort Huachuca, he stopped in Phoenix to view his brother's progress.

George Scott had arrived in Phoenix in December 1888. Pitching a tent on the southwest corner of Section 23, he began the arduous task of clearing the greasewood and digging the irrigation ditches. By late February he had completed the planting of eighty acres of barley, a twenty-acre vineyard, and a seven-acre orchard. Ornamental trees were planted outlining the southwest quarter section of the property with an additional row planted through the center. It is obvious that George Scott did not accomplish this dazzling progress alone, but only the name of Bert Spencer has surfaced as a possible hired hand. Perhaps the nearby Pimas helped. They would work for Chaplain Scott in the years to come, harvesting his crops, and it is a distinct possibility that they were enlisted at this early date. In any event, George had accomplished a great deal by the time his brother arrived, and, in a real sense, George Scott was Scottsdale's first citizen in residence.

Chaplain Scott arranged his trip from Angel Island to Fort Huachuca to coincide with a series of revival meetings held at the Phoenix Baptist Church, and after assisting there, he filled the pulpit of the Presbyterian church for two Sunday services before continuing on to his new station. George Scott used the opportunity of his brother's visit to come to town, and he stayed at the Commercial Hotel on Center Street. The clean sheets and hotel cooking must have seemed like paradise to the desert camper. Chaplain Scott utilized this time in Phoenix not only to preach and inspect his property, but also to attend to several legal matters. In the Maricopa County Recorder's office, he filed his agreement with the Arizona Canal Company transferring seven water rights in the Arizona Canal to his land.* Having given legal notice of his efforts to secure water for his land, he filed, with the clerk of the United States District Court in Phoenix, his disposition of final proof detailing the steps he had taken to reclaim his property from the desert. The next day, again in the recorder's office, he filed a warranty deed conveying forty acres of his land and one-half of a water right to Mary Brown White of Rochester, New York, for thirty dollars an acre. Once again, Winfield Scott was strengthening the Scott family tradition of acuity in real estate transactions. It is probable that he sold those forty acres in order to meet his financial obligations, but he was able to make a handsome profit on the transaction. Having put his affairs in order in the Salt River Valley, Chaplain Scott moved on to his new station.

The Apache wars had been over for two and a half years when Winfield Scott reported to Fort Huachuca in March 1889. Situated some dozen miles from the Mexican border in southeast Arizona, the fort had served as a base to intercept Apache raiding parties both entering and leaving the United States and also played an important role in protecting the civilian population of the area.[5] Now, however, routine patrols replaced constant readiness, and Scott began his program of Sunday school in the morning and preaching in the evening

---

*Each water right entitled the holder to buy water to irrigate 80 acres. The discrepancy between Scott's purchase of rights covering 560 acres and his desert land claim to 640 acres is explained by the path of the Arizona Canal through the northwest quarter section of his property. The route of the canal separated between 67 and 72 acres which lay north of the canal from the bulk of the section which lay south of it. It was not possible for Scott to irrigate those acres which lay north of the canal, as they were higher than the waterway, and he therefore did not purchase a water right for them. He relinquished his claim to the northwest quarter of the northwest quarter section containing 40 acres but kept the remaining 27 to 32 acres north of the canal. Why he relinquished some acres and kept others is not clear. In any event, the remaining 88 to 93 acres in the northwest quarter section south of the canal were covered by water right number 263 which was to irrigate "as much of the northwest quarter as lies under the canal being eighty acres more or less."

Fort Huachuca, Arizona Territory. View looking north from the mouth of Central (Post) Canyon in the northeast end of the Huachuca Mountains. (Quartermaster General Photograph, National Archives)

with an occasional lecture added for good measure. Since there were so few ministers in the neighborhood, Scott once again attended to the marrying and burying of the civilian population. As at Angel Island, he acted as school superintendent overseeing both the school for the post children and the school for the enlisted men. In addition, he found time to continue his zealous "chamber of commerce" activities on behalf of the Salt River Valley.

In June he wrote a long letter to the Boston *Watchman,* a Baptist publication, detailing the advantages of Arizona in general and the Salt River Valley in particular. Admitting that Arizona was known as "the porch of perdition" and "the paradise of rattlesnakes, gila monsters and Apaches," Scott bid the tourist to visit the Salt River Valley saying, "I have been twenty-four years now in the west, living in nearly all the states from the Missouri River to the Pacific Coast, and I can say without reserve that I have never seen a land of greater fertility or richer promise."

Having initiated his first planting of fifty orange trees the previous winter, Chaplain Scott took a leave of absence in October to oversee the beginning of his second experiment with citrus. On the basis of his past experience in California, he strongly suspected that the orange would thrive in the valley of the Salt, and he intended to make commercial citrus production a major focus on his ranch. At the same time that George Scott planted the first fifty trees, the Arizona Improvement Company also decided to experiment with citrus. A mile and a half to the west of Scott's ranch it planted sixteen acres in oranges and a few in lemons.* Previous to this time, individuals had grown a few orange trees in their backyards, but there had been no commercial orchards. These initial experiments of Scott and the Arizona Improvement Company signaled the beginning of commercial citrus production in the Salt River Valley.

The Improvement Company stood to gain handsomely if the commercial production of citrus proved to be successful. Headed by William J. Murphy, it controlled the four major irrigation canals north of the Salt River and owned "much of the finest land in the valley." New citrus farmers, encouraged by the company's hoped for success, would

---

*In March 1889 Luther G. Dorris, recently arrived from Winona, Mississippi, supervised a crew of men in planting the Improvement Company's first citrus orchard of thirteen hundred trees. Dorris lived with his wife and six-year-old daughter in a frame tent house near the bank of the Arizona Canal, and Dorris's daughter Veronica remembers that water flowed in the canal only at certain times, spaced perhaps as far apart as every eight days. When water flowed, Dorris filled several barrels for the use of his family and crew and irrigated his sixteen acres of trees. His wife thoroughly despised living in the unshaded desert, and shortly after the first oranges were picked in November 1891, she persuaded her husband to return to Mississippi. Luther G. Dorris, nevertheless, has the distinction of being the first cultivator and manager of a commercial citrus orchard in the Salt River Valley.

be in the market for its properties, and new citrus farms would greatly expand the use of its canals. The orange trees purchased by the company were "two-year-old buds on three-year-old roots brought balled and sacked from Southern California." The harvest of the first crop began November 10, 1891, and except for its abnormally large size, the fruit was critically judged to be excellent in every regard. The company's initial experiment was a great success.

Scott's initial experiment had also been a success, as only three trees failed to survive. His second experiment, however, undertaken two years before the Improvement Company's first harvest, proved to be of greater significance. On his October leave he supervised the planting of fifteen hundred orange trees. These new trees, in contrast with the considerably more mature trees of the Improvement Company, were brought from California as six-inch seedlings. Doubting Thomases predicted disaster. They said that mature trees might withstand frost unharmed but not these tiny seedlings. Scott, nevertheless, had faith in the favorable climate of his location. The dry air was of definite benefit as was the protection afforded by the east end of Camelback Mountain. His tiny trees survived the winters of 1889–1890 and 1890–1891 unprotected and without harm. The winter of 1891–1892 proved to be an unusually cold one, and the record low temperatures were a rude revelation. As early as December 6, the temperature dipped to twenty degrees in Phoenix and dropped to twelve degrees on Christmas Eve. Some orchards planted the previous spring were frozen to the ground, but the temperature in the burgeoning "orange belt" along Camelback Mountain remained just high enough to save the trees. Scott had been right. His location had proved to be safe for citrus in even the most unforeseen cold, and as a result, his experiment was a success. He had established beyond question that citrus could be grown commercially from seedlings in the Salt River Valley.

During that October leave in 1889, Scott also visited the county recorder to file the receipt for his final payment made under the Desert Land Act. The payment, made in September at the land office in Tucson, amounted to $1,200, representing $2 an acre for 600 acres. His initial sale, seven months earlier, of 40 acres for $30 an acre covered this final payment, but Scott had many other obligations to meet and found it necessary to sell additional acreage. His water rights alone probably cost him three times the amount of his final payment; it is likely he borrowed money to pay for them, and they only guaranteed him the right to buy water from the canal company. In addition, bills for fruit trees, barley seed, grapevines, water, supplies, and three miles of fence needed payment, and for these reasons it is probable that Scott entered into negotiations with W. J. Murphy. On October 30, 1889, he

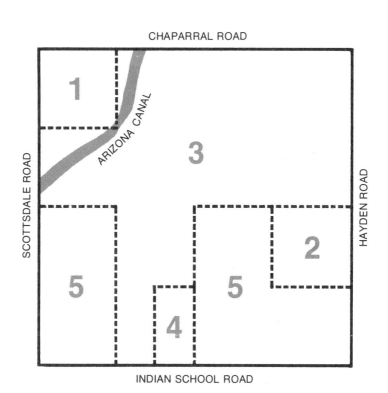

DISPOSITION OF SCOTT'S SECTION
1888–1893

CHAPARRAL ROAD

ARIZONA CANAL

SCOTTSDALE ROAD

HAYDEN ROAD

INDIAN SCHOOL ROAD

1. Returned to U.S. Government

2. Sold to Mary Brown White

3. Sold to W. J. Murphy

4. Repurchased from W. J. Murphy

5. Retained by Scott

sold Murphy 360 acres of his section for $25 an acre.* Scott farmed his remaining 200 acres until 1908.

While in Phoenix on his nine-day October leave, it is also highly probable that Scott visited his daughter Minnie. A recent graduate of the Chicago Kindergarten Institute, Minnie had been hired to teach for the fall term in the new East End School in Phoenix. The opportunity to be close to her parents probably influenced Minnie's decision to return west, but by the spring of 1890 it seemed that being close no longer sufficed. Before the end of the school term, Minnie suddenly left Phoenix to join her parents at Fort Huachuca. The *Phoenix Herald* reported that she had left due to her father's illness, but this cannot be verified, because Scott's monthly letters to the adjutant general from March 1890 to June 1891 are missing. It seems likely, however, that the purported illness was an excuse, for in the fall Minnie did not return to Phoenix, and the reason given was her need for a year's rest. In any event, a return to family and post life agreed with Minnie, and she soon met a young lieutenant who would become her husband.

By the spring of 1890 Scott had twenty-five hundred trees in his nursery, his vineyard covered forty-five acres, and he planned to put in forty acres of navel and Mediterranean orange trees, grown in Florida but budded in Sacramento, California. The apricot and peach trees which had been cut to within fifteen inches of the ground in the winter of 1889 were thriving, as were the almond and nectarine trees. Of the one hundred Monterrey cypress trees brought from California as two-inch seedlings, eighty survived to line the border of the Scott ranch. In addition, the palm, umbrella, and pepper trees planted that first winter continued their unabated growth. By the late 1890s, when the summer sun made it too hot to hold church services indoors, the chaplain's shady grove would be used as the place of worship. It seems appropriate that his avocation of husbanding the land should so pleasantly assist his calling.

When Scott came to inspect his ranch in the fall of 1890, he stopped in Phoenix to visit an old college friend, Freeman D. Rickerson, pastor of the First Baptist Church. Rickerson and Scott had been at Rochester together thirty years before, and only recently their paths had crossed again in California where Scott found his fellow Baptist in failing health. The chaplain persuaded Rickerson to come to the Salt River Valley to try to regain his strength, and in April 1889 the Reverend Dr.

---

*Out of his section, Scott sold Murphy the northeast quarter (160 acres), the east half of the southwest quarter (80 acres), and the east half and the southwest quarter of the northwest quarter (120 acres). This left Scott with two noncontiguous parcels of 80 acres (the west half of the southwest quarter) and 120 acres (the west half and the southeast quarter of the southeast quarter). He also farmed Mary Brown White's 40 acres (the northeast quarter of the southeast quarter), which meant that Scott farmed the entire southeast quarter section until purchased by Charles Miller in 1908.

View looking west on Washington Street, Phoenix, ca. 1890. Henry E. Kemp's hardware store in the left middle ground was located on Montezuma (First Street) across from city hall. The three-story building to the left and rear of Kemp's store is the Commercial Hotel (today's Luhrs Hotel) which fronted on Center Street (Central Avenue) and which was the hotel where Scott and his brother often stayed on trips to town. (Historical Collection of Herb and Dorothy McLaughlin, Phoenix, Arizona)

Rickerson became missionary pastor to the Phoenix Baptists. Under his capable guidance, Rickerson's congregation first remodeled and then rebuilt their church. With the financial assistance of his former congregations and the American Baptist Home Mission Society, they paid off the church debt and in early March 1892 proudly became a self-supporting congregation. The cost proved exceedingly high, however, as the worry and strain of three years of fund raising and rebuilding taxed the limits of what strength Rickerson had regained. His health failed him completely, and he died March 29, 1892. Chaplain Scott came up from Fort Huachuca to conduct the funeral service and had a difficult time completing his remarks. It was a happier time on that September leave in 1890, with Scott staying in Rickerson's home, and before returning to Fort Huachuca, he preached to his friend's congregation.

This scene would be repeated many times during the next two years as Scott's reputation as a speaker and a preacher became well established in the valley. Whenever he came up to inspect his ranch, a church in Phoenix, Tempe, or Mesa prevailed upon him to fill its pulpit. Sometimes he could even be persuaded to preach in Phoenix in the morning and Tempe in the evening. Between attending to his ranch and preaching, every minute of every furlough was utilized. Whether it was not in his makeup to say no or whether he enjoyed his hectic pace, it is undeniable that the man seemed to draw on an undiminishing source of energy.

On March 4, 1891, Minnie Scott married Lieutenant Frank H. Albright in her parents' quarters at Fort Huachuca. Beneath a canopy of flags, white lilacs, and roses, Chaplain Scott united his eldest daughter and her lieutenant in matrimony. It was a high point in a year in which Scott would make special efforts to help fill the free time of his charges. He donned the editor's hat once again and began to publish the *Huachuca Sentinel,* a weekly, four-page, two-column paper written for the soldiers and civilians of the fort. He organized a literary society to provide lectures, debates, and light entertainment. A dramatic club and a singing class were also fostered by Scott. Recognizing the need for physical as well as mental stimulation, he requested that a building on the post be converted into a gymnasium. What manner of success he enjoyed in these efforts is not known, but regardless of success or failure, he made the extra effort.

Away to the northwest the orchards and vineyards of Scott's desert ranch continued to thrive. During the winter of 1890–1891 an additional twenty-eight acres were planted in oranges, and ten acres were added to the vineyard. Seven varieties of grapes for both table use and raisin production were now under cultivation. In addition to the oranges, apricots, peaches, almonds, and nectarines, Scott was experimenting with pears, plums, figs, lemons, apples, and cherries. In the coming years most of these experiments proved successful from the standpoint of actual fruit production,* but along the way, the forces of nature and the cutthroat practices of the marketplace dealt Scott serious setbacks. Breaks in the Arizona Canal at inopportune times, a severe drought in the late 1890s, and prices for fruit which did not even pay the freight charges caused the chaplain severe losses. He responded by continuing to experiment with different fruits and crops until he had the right combination to make his ranch profitable. By the end of his life this meant that his orchards and vineyard had been reduced to only a handful of acres and that alfalfa covered the rest of his land. In the process of making his ranch a paying proposition, however, and before the drought destroyed his years of effort, he established an economic base for the community that was to grow up around his property.

In October 1891 Scott traveled to California to purchase orange trees for the winter planting. He visited the W. R. Strong Company in Sacramento to order trees from their Florida nursery. He also made arrangements to assure himself of a supply of first-class trees for a new sideline. Recently he had purchased several thousand trees for friends, and it was a simple step from there to selling citrus trees to the public. Scott placed advertisements in the *Phoenix Herald* offering five thousand orange and lemon trees for sale in lots ranging from one hundred trees for seventy cents apiece to one thousand trees for sixty cents each. After only ten days a second advertisement appeared offering twenty-five thousand trees for sale. When he paid a visit to the valley in December, he once again placed an advertisement for twenty-five thousand trees and indicated he would be taking orders at the Valley Bank. It is not clear whether Scott sold all fifty-five thousand trees or whether the subsequent advertisements offered trees not previously sold, but whatever the situation, it is clear that Scott was determined to help make the Salt River Valley the orange capital of the West.

Chaplain Scott never stopped promoting his adopted home. He convinced a fellow officer at Fort Huachuca to invest in a one-hundred-acre tract near his ranch and helped him plant it in oranges and lemons. When a devastating flood struck the Salt River Valley in February

---

*In 1913, when Charles Miller bought the eighty acres containing Scott's orchards and vineyard, he found apricot, peach, pear, plum, fig, almond, lemon, orange, and grapefruit trees still thriving and producing more fruit than the Millers and their friends could eat. Miller also found two rows of grapevines about two football fields in length which contained "so many varieties of grapes" that they probably contained the seven varieties Scott originally planted. All told, Scott's once proud and famous orchards and vineyard now covered less than ten acres, but the fruit they produced was still reportedly beautiful and delicious.

1891, Scott penned a letter to the New York *Evangelist*, a leading Baptist newspaper. He acknowledged that the flood had caused a great deal of damage but added that the rain had not been all bad, as it saved the crops after a dry fall and winter. Although "the few have lost their hundreds, the great valley is richer by its hundreds of thousands." In addition, Scott went on, the flood clearly indicated where to build and plant in the future. The high-water mark had left its message.

It was typical of Scott to put this face on the situation. It has been said by one who knew him that he was eternally optimistic. Throughout his own various misfortunes, he was calm and cheerful. He would rub his bald head a few times, say that things would get better, and go on. His neighbors found strength in his serenity, and the local newspapers appreciated his spirit. His letter on the flood, which also contained descriptions of the Salt River Valley's fertility and its extensive irrigation canal system, apparently sparked a wave of interest in the valley, especially among easterners who had considered Arizona a vast, waterless desert. After Scott's letter, the Phoenix Chamber of Commerce began to receive inquiries concerning business opportunities in the valley. Scott had turned adversity to advantage. It was a bold stroke, in keeping with his character, and indicative of his determination to share his home with as many people as would listen.

In 1892 Scott began one of his experiments that proved highly successful; he began raising peanuts. Scott was a firm believer that land should pay for itself, but his orchard of tiny orange trees would not generate an income for several years. In fact, a considerable expense was entailed in irrigating, weeding, and pruning the orchard. In an effort to remedy this situation, Scott bought premium peanut seed at the Citrus Fair in Los Angeles. The first year this prize-winning seed was planted to generate more seed, but the following spring, Scott planted his first cash crop, one row of peanuts between each row of orange trees.

In November 1893 Winfield Scott harvested the first commercial crop of peanuts in Arizona Territory. Employing his Pima neighbors for the harvest, his experiment yielded twenty-five hundred pounds of nuts. Retaining five hundred pounds for seed, he filled a wagon with sacks containing the rest. At the Phoenix market, Scott sold the wagonload to Charles Donofrio for five cents a pound—$100. Donofrio, who owned a fruit and candy store, had bought the crop to encourage a new Arizona industry. Not expecting to sell the peanuts in a year's time, he was back to see Scott in six weeks. The peanuts were gone, and he wanted more. The income from the sale to Donofrio covered the cost of maintaining the citrus nursery for one year. Not only that but the pragmatic preacher found that his farm animals preferred peanut

Charles Donofrio in front of his fruit and confectionery store on East Washington Street. (Historical Collection of Herb and Dorothy McLaughlin, Phoenix, Arizona)

Arizona peanuts on the vine. (Historical Collection of Herb and Dorothy McLaughlin, Phoenix, Arizona) vines to alfalfa. The next year Scott harvested five tons of peanuts and covered his expenses many times over. He had been successful not only in making his nursery pay for itself, but also in developing a new cash crop. He was not finished, however, with experiments in his citrus nursery.

The record cold temperatures of the winter of 1891–1892 indicated that even in the "orange belt" of the Salt River Valley citrus should be protected. Scott decided to experiment with a method similar to one used in California. Between the rows of orange trees and peanut plants he drilled rows of Egyptian corn.* The corn was planted in July and harvested in December. After Scott sold the grain, which yielded fifty to sixty bushels to the acre, he wrapped the husks around the tree trunks for protection against frost. At the end of the winter the husks were removed and chopped into fodder. Scott was an innovative yet frugal farmer, and nowhere is that better illustrated than in his citrus nursery.

In April 1892 the headquarters of the Eleventh Infantry and most of the garrison left Fort Huachuca for Fort Whipple near Prescott. Six companies remained including one Indian and three black. This greatly reduced garrison meant a significant decline in the chaplain's congregation, but what concerned him more than this was the sale of beer and malt liquor to the troops. He was especially concerned for the Indians and blacks who had the greatest problems with alcohol and who spent the most time in the guardhouse because of it. The Indians, who were allowed to buy beer in direct conflict with civil law, became involved in so many altercations related to drunkeness, that they were soon prohibited from purchasing any alcohol. Scott was not satisfied, however, and "respectfully but urgently" recommended in a monthly report to the adjutant general that "all beer and malt liquor be prohibited at the exchange." He reminded the adjutant general of the large number of summary and general courts-martial at Fort Huachuca and closed by saying he had "good reason to believe that liquor is the prime cause of nearly all." In an effort to have an immediate impact on the situation, Scott promoted the organization of a temperance society and assisted at its weekly meeting. He was a dedicated prohibitionist and would continue in temperance work all his life. Being a pragmatic man, he must have wondered if the continual confrontation with an indifferent and sometimes hostile society was worth the effort, but Winfield Scott never skirted a fight if he felt the cause was just.

In late 1892 Chaplain Scott's old Civil War wounds brought to a

---

*Lest the reader think that the nursery was getting crowded, citrus orchards in those early days were planted with rows twenty-five feet apart. There was ample room for trees, vines, and stalks.

halt his ten years of military service. For many years he had suffered from numbness and cramping in his right leg, and for the past year and a half he had been unable to walk or ride horseback for more than a few minutes without experiencing intense pain and severe cramping. His right leg was a mass of varicose veins and atrophied muscle, and by late 1892 the tissues of the limb had become so inflamed that the post surgeon feared imminent ulceration. He ordered a six-month leave of absence, justified by a certificate of medical disability. Except for the formality of his appearance before an army retirement board in the summer of 1893, Chaplain Winfield Scott's military career was at an end. Once more he had served his country well. He had done his duty; he had given the extra measure; and all the while he had lived with his pain. Saying good-bye to his wife and daughter who would join him later, Scott headed for the Salt River Valley. Although his peripatetic sojourns were not over, his ranch under the lee of the Arizona Canal would be home for the rest of his life.

Young, bearing orange orchard in the lee of Camelback Mountain. Note the wide spacing between the rows which allowed Scott ample room to plant his peanuts and corn. (Historical Collection of Herb and Dorothy McLaughlin, Phoenix, Arizona)

CHAPTER IX

The Scottsdale Townsite

Even before receiving a medical leave of absence, Winfield Scott made plans to fill his days of "rest." In December 1892 in a *Phoenix Herald* article, he announced a new service for individuals who bought land in his neighborhood. For a fee, which the newspaper termed reasonable, Scott offered these individuals one- to three-year contracts to plant and care for groves set out on their property. While the *Herald* lauded Scott's horticultural expertise, most of the landowners in his neighborhood were not interested in developing their land with orchards, and the first known contract was not signed until two years later. Nevertheless, from Scott's point of view, the idea had merit. In the coming months he would have ample time to attend to his own orchards and any others he could develop under contract.

Having been instructed to rest when he reached the Salt River Valley, Scott disobeyed his doctor's orders with abandon. Upon arriving in Phoenix in late January 1893, he took delivery of his first orange trees of the season, a carload of seven thousand from Florida. He planted two thousand trees in his own grove and sold the rest to growers. Two weeks later the next carload of trees arrived, and Scott put them on display on Washington Street between Second and Third Avenues. C. D. Light, of Gila Bend, purchased twelve hundred trees from this second lot; Colonel William Christy, the territorial treasurer, vice-president of the Arizona Improvement Company, and Valley Bank cashier, bought fifteen hundred trees; and Christy's son George came forward with a timely testimonial. The young farmer, who would go on to command a company of the Rough Riders during the Spanish-American War and who would later become a Phoenix attorney,[1] stated to the *Herald* that out of the twelve hundred trees he had purchased from Scott the year before, only three had died. Good quality stock and what the newspaper termed "lower rates than ever was known in the valley" proved a profitable combination. The Arizona Improvement Company, the Valley Bank, and several individual growers kept Scott busy with their orders.

Perhaps feeling it better to introduce his wife and daughter gradually to ranch life in the desert, Scott planned to live in Phoenix for awhile, and in preparation for their arrival, purchased a lot and built a home in the Brill Addition to Phoenix. To make an early move to the ranch plausible, he supervised the digging of a well and fortuitously struck soft water at sixty feet.* In partnership with M. E. Gillet, Scott purchased back 20 of the 360 acres he had sold to W. J. Murphy in 1889 and made plans to plant them in oranges and sell them as two 10-acre groves. With his wife Helen, who arrived in Phoenix in early March, he helped organize the Arizona Baptist Association. Formerly affiliated with the Baptist organization of Southern California, the Arizona churches formed their own group and held their first meeting with the Scotts' guidance. What makes this activity remarkable is that it all occurred within two months of his arrival in the valley. It is quite possible that constant activity took his mind off the pain. Either that or Winfield Scott did not know how to slow down and rest.

In the spring Scott planted four thousand orange trees, some of which he added to the nursery stock in preparation to selling trees from his own grove in the fall. With his third crop of grapes and apricots nearing maturity, and as Memorial Day approached, Scott took the opportunity to preach in the Presbyterian church in Phoenix. Memorial Day held a special significance for Scott, because it honored his fallen comrades, and many old soldiers and sons of veterans came to hear him. Although his remarks routinely received praise, many of his listeners came away that day saying his address was the finest of its kind they had ever heard. Shortly thereafter, Scott was named chaplain of the National Guard of Arizona. It was not his lot to lead a quiet life.

The apricots and grapes were harvested in June and July, and Scott publicized the event by bringing baskets full of both fruits to the office of the *Herald*. Such generosity did not go unnoticed in the columns of the paper. He harvested at least two carloads of table grapes that summer and sold them to wholesale buyers Dobson and Root who shipped them by refrigerator car to Chicago. A new market had been opened for Scott, and his grapes returned "$30 per ton or about $250 per acre."

---

*Before the turn of the century and into the early decades of this century, finding soft water in shallow strata proved to be the rule rather than the exception in the Scottsdale area.

When Chaplain Scott requested an extension of his leave of absence in late July 1893, the commanding general of the Department of Arizona ordered him before an army retirement board. Upon hearing the testimony of the surgeons involved and of Scott himself, and upon examination of the leg, the board ordered him furloughed pending his replacement and retirement. There is no question that Winfield Scott was medically unfit for further active service, but the question remains: why did he force the issue before a retirement board? If he could maintain a demanding schedule in pursuit of his personal business, why did he request an extension of his medical leave? Why did he not return to duty? There is no question that he lived in constant pain. Perhaps he was tired of bearing that pain in order to benefit others. Perhaps his growing infirmity caused him to reassess his priorities. Seeing a better life evolving on his desert ranch, perhaps he sought a way out of his commitment. Scott was, after all, only human. In surveying the course of Winfield Scott's life, it is reassuring to get an occasional glimpse of his humanity.

In the fall Scott spent a good deal of time supplying the pulpits of the Tempe and Phoenix Baptist churches. When the pastor of the Phoenix church became ill, Scott stepped in to conduct a series of revival services. His presence, when announced in the newspaper, drew a number of the leading citizens of Phoenix to the first meeting. Scott's reputation as a lively and interesting speaker drew listeners across ordinary denominational lines. In addition to his preaching, Scott planted several thousand fruit and shade trees, harvested his first crop of peanuts, and advertised the sale of five thousand orange trees from his nursery. A sack of sweet potatoes left at the *Herald* office signaled another harvest and another successful experiment.

It was a busy fall for Scott, but he was not too busy to offer assistance to a young man from Denver. The young man's name was Merton Tuckee, an electrician by trade, who had come to the valley to regain his health. Scott gave him a place to stay on the ranch, and the temperate climate of the valley seemed to be the right tonic. For several weeks he improved; then, suddenly, he caught cold and died. A recurrence of hemorrhaging in his lungs proved too much for his system. Merton Tuckee was but the first of scores of people who were to live with the Scotts. Some were ill, others were down on their luck, and still others were looking for a fresh start in a new land. Some experienced the chaplain's generosity, while others paid their way as winter boarders. In the home that Scott built on his ranch and in tents pitched in his shady grove, people from all over the country stayed until they could get started on their own. This was the beginning of a community.

Just south of Scott's ranch was a section of land owned by Rhode

Chaplain Scott with his wife Helen seated on Old Maud. A veteran of the Apache campaigns, Old Maud retired with Scott when he left Fort Huachuca in January, 1893. (Mrs. Elsie Elliott Severance, Calexico, California)

Island banker Albert G. Utley.* In February 1894 plans were announced to subdivide the northwest forty acres of that section into a townsite called Orangedale. In conjunction with George A. Williams, "a prominent citizen of Chicago" who owned the adjacent forty acres on the west, Utley planned to develop a residential community for individuals who would work in Phoenix and live in Orangedale. Plans included a street railway line to accommodate these new commuters, and in the interim, a "daily bus line" would be run to Phoenix. The plans also included a sanatorium for people with respiratory problems, a complex of small homes to be rented by winter visitors, and a large resort hotel. The name Orangedale was chosen to associate the town with the growing "orange belt" south of the Arizona Canal along the length of Camelback Mountain, and Chaplain Winfield Scott was to "have charge of the enterprise."

In addition to the developers' plans, Scott intended to colonize the area to the north and east of the townsite with farmers who would plant new orchards and vineyards. The *Herald* praised the innovative chap-

*In June 1890 Albert G. Utley bought the section immediately south of Scott's property from his niece, Nannie C. Utley Fulwiler, for $1,000.

lain for his work in successfully growing many varieties of fruit beyond the experimental stage and in summarizing the townsite idea, said of Scott, "To his energy and devotion to the interests of that part of the valley is largely due the founding of this town." Sometime between February and August of 1894, for reasons that are not known but which certainly had to do with recognition of Scott's role in "the founding of this town," the name of the townsite was changed from Orangedale to Scottsdale. The little community that was to grow up around Scott's ranch had taken on a form. It remained for him to give it substance.

It was announced that townsite preparations would be thorough and that lots would go on sale in 1895. In the meantime, Scott had other commitments to meet. As vice-president of the Maricopa County Horticultural Society, he was selected to give the welcoming address to a large group of Ohio farmers on a tour of the Southwest. That same organization also asked him to prepare a paper on the question "Is Arizona adapted to the growth of citrus fruits?"

In February the pastor of the Phoenix Baptist Church resigned, and Scott was once again prevailed upon to serve until a new minister could be found. In addition to his Sunday morning services, he presented a series of lectures to young businessmen. The themes of his lectures, "The Young Man Away from Home," "Investments," "Brain, Force, and Conscience," and the old favorite from Denver days "Gambling," suggest that a strong strain of the social gospel was still prevalent in the Scott ministry.

In April the convention of the Arizona Baptist Association elected Scott moderator and appointed him to the group's mission board for the coming year. While the Baptists met in Tempe, Scott was called upon to preach in the Tempe church in the morning and to lecture in Phoenix in the evening. His invitations to speak around the valley seemed to come without pause. As a final responsibility, Scott was appointed to a committee to organize a Maricopa County Farmers Institute. He fulfilled all these duties while having a record year harvesting grapes, apricots, and peanuts.

Soon after the announcement of the Orangedale townsite plan, Scott stopped off at the *Herald* with a crate of raisins from his ranch. Dried from grapes harvested the year before, they were pronounced by the newspaper to be "equal in quality to anything in the general markets." This first substantial production of raisins augured well for the future and spelled the beginning of an intensified crop cultivation that would eventually produce twenty tons of raisins for Scott in one season.[2]

During the second week in May 1894 Scott checked his early apricots and found to his surprise that he should have been picking them for the past four days. He quickly hired a gang of men and was soon shipping fifty to one hundred boxes a day to markets in Arizona, New Mexico, Colorado, Texas, and California. The apricots were of the "Newcastle Early" variety, and the name was quite appropriate. Many were shipped to San Diego and Los Angeles, and sending apricots to Southern California was indeed analogous to carrying coals to Newcastle. Scott captured the early market because his apricots were several weeks ahead of the California crop. One of the selling points that Scott had made for six years in promoting the Salt River Valley was the market advantage to be gained by its early ripening fruit. His apricots gave telling testimony in support of this contention.

By late May Scott's "Royal" variety of apricots were ready to be harvested and yielded a total crop of fifteen thousand pounds. Most were bound for Texas, but ever the one to experiment, Scott sent fifteen crates to New Orleans to see how they would stand the trip. They arrived in excellent condition and brought three dollars a box. Letters soon reached Scott from the Texas markets congratulating him on his apricots. They had proven to be the best of the season and had been quickly sold out. Such praise did not help bring in the crops, however, and Scott proceeded with preparations to harvest his ripening grapes.

By June 14 a railroad car was en route to Phoenix carrying wooden boxes consigned to Scott for the grape harvest. By July 9 his first shipment, 135 boxes, left for Tucson. Soon thereafter, he hired an additional force of men, and the harvest began in earnest. The first carload left for Kansas City July 25, containing 1,030 boxes of Muscat of Alexandria grapes and 11,000 pounds of ice. The next day the first carload left for Chicago. Scott's early grapes reached the Chicago market before any others, and while he had the market to himself he received six cents a pound. When grapes from other states finally reached the market, the price was halved. Scott's grapes joined his apricots in telling the Salt River Valley story.

Winfield Scott was quite fortunate that summer of 1894, for none of his many shipments was halted or delayed by the Pullman railway strike. Many fruit shippers lost heavily when Eugene V. Debs and his American Railway Union kept traffic snarled for months. Scott's own misfortune came in early September when his partner in the fruit-shipping business, C. B. Richman, departed the valley rather suddenly with the books and accounts of the partnership. Richman's departure was as abrupt as his arrival, and nothing more is known of this phantom partner. It can only be surmised that Scott's loss was significant. Without any more acknowledgment of his personal disaster than a published warning not to accept drafts on the "dissolved" partnership, Scott resumed his agricultural activities.

The peanut harvest in late November capped a year of agricultural successes for Scott. Approximately five tons of nuts were taken to market, where Clay Leonard, another Phoenix confectioner and fruit dealer, bought the whole crop. At about this same time, Scott came to Phoenix to make arrangements to open the Scottsdale townsite for sale in the coming winter. An idea was coming closer to realization. It remained for Scott to finish the year by harvesting his corn and fig crops. The Arizona Improvement Company was then preparing an exhibit of valley products for display in Chicago, and Scott supplied specimens of each of his late fall crops. It took colossal self-assurance to send Arizona corn to Chicago, but Winfield Scott seldom missed an opportunity to advertise the fertility of the Salt River Valley.

When Dr. James M. Ford of Kansas City, Missouri, signed a one-year contract with Scott to plant and care for a forty-acre orange grove, it signaled a good beginning to the year 1895. It was Scott's first known contract to farm for absentee owners, but more than that it helped publicize a growing interest in the new Scottsdale townsite. In early March the first Scottsdale advertisement appeared in the *Phoenix Herald*. In bold-face type was proclaimed

SCOTTSDALE FRUIT LANDS
NEW TOWN JUST STARTING!

The advertisement detailed the agricultural potential of the area, the many fruits that were already growing there, and the opportunity to buy either undeveloped acreage or orchards nearing maturity. For health seekers, the advertisement declared that the surgeon general of Arizona, Dr. Scott Helm, and other prominent physicians certified Scottsdale to be "the Best Location for Sanitary purposes of any part of the valley." Included also was the timeless line of real estate promotion, "Land in tracts to suit at reasonable prices and on easy terms." Gone were the early pretentions of a resort hotel, street railway line, and the complex of winter homes; instead, the pragmatic, down-to-earth hand of Winfield Scott is seen.

During 1894 the people who had shown an interest in Scottsdale had been health seekers and individuals interested in agricultural land. There had been a railway man from Kansas City and a grain merchant from Chicago who spent the winter on Scott's ranch, hunting duck and quail in the nearby slough, hunting jackrabbits with Scott's pack of greyhounds, and trying to regain their health. There had been a fruit dealer from Minneapolis who had been so impressed with the orchards of Scott, W. J. Murphy, and Henry E. Kemp that he had decided to invest in Scottsdale land. Finally, there had been an increasing interest in the valley in general, and the Scottsdale area in particular, by farmers interested in citrus ranching. The experiments of the Arizona Improvement Company and its president William J. Murphy, of Winfield Scott, and of men such as W. M. Ward and Henry E. Kemp had taken citrus in the Salt River Valley from an idea to an industry. By 1894 the valley contained fifteen hundred acres of oranges, lemons, and limes. Scott had played a major role in the birth of this new industry, and he was moving now to capitalize on its growing popularity by advertising the citrus potential in Scottsdale.

With Scott spending an increasing amount of time in the promotion of the townsite, his brother George returned from San Francisco to once again manage the ranch. He had been gone since 1891, and why he had left at that time is not known. He was back now, however, and the *Herald* recognized him as the "founder of the Chaplain Scott ranch." It seemed a time for family reunion that spring. Helen Scott Flint brought her two children down from Oakland to visit their grandparents. Old Maud, an army mule which Scott had brought with him from Fort Huachuca, and Old Bob, a ranch horse, were not being used to pull the harvest wagons just yet, and it is more than likely they were pressed into service as mounts for the grandchildren. In later years, when they were too old for farm work, Scott instructed the farmhands to leave them be, and they became the companions and trusty steeds of the children of Scottsdale.

Agricultural accomplishments were once again significant in the year's activities. The early apricots were unusually early, and Scott was shipping to Chicago by May 13. It was gratifying to be so early; that had been one of his original intentions in selecting his valley location. In point of fact, he had chosen quite well. Not only was Scott reaching eastern markets first, but he was also first to pick his fruit in the Salt River Valley. That summer his vineyards were especially prolific, with the resulting production of raisins enormous. In addition to his usual shipments of table grapes, he marketed ten tons of raisins. On a much smaller scale, he succeeded with yet another experiment. Harking back to his Kansas days, he decided to plant potatoes. The harvest proved successful, and he sold the crop in the Phoenix market. He also presented some choice specimens to the Phoenix Chamber of Commerce. Here was further proof of the valley's fertility with which to entice the prospective western immigrant. These successes are only a small sample of the many accomplishments that were gaining Scott a growing reputation in the Arizona agricultural community. In the fall of 1895 his contributions to Arizona agriculture were acknowledged at the organizational meeting of the Arizona Agricultural Association. He was unanimously elected the group's vice-president. For a man who had lived in the community just two years, this was recognition of a high order.

The week before Christmas 1895 a tragic fire occurred on the Scott ranch. While the Scotts and their boarders were at breakfast in a separate building, the main house erupted in flame. How the fire started in the frame structure is not known, but by the time anyone realized what was happening, the home was engulfed in flames. A burning trunk with its charred contents was all that was saved. The Scotts and their boarders were left with only the clothes they were wearing. Scott's books and papers were his treasures. He had moved them across a continent and part way back again, adding as he traveled from one appointment to another. Having to pack and unpack his library at least seventeen times is indicative of its value to Scott. Now it lay in ashes. Helen Scott, too, was bereft of her treasures, a few reminders of her New York home. It has been said that she never reconciled herself to living in the desert. Her ongoing adjustment would be more difficult now without those things that made her home more comfortable. A life's accumulation of papers, momentos, photographs, and letters went up in smoke. It was a traumatic loss for the Scotts. They would have to begin anew, and many things could never be replaced.

With each succeeding year Winfield Scott became more involved in the affairs of his valley. He chaired a committee appointed by the Arizona Agricultural Association to help secure better markets for the fruits of the Salt River Valley. Realizing from personal experience that in the shipment of fresh fruit, the small grower was at the mercy of eastern commission agents and local wholesale shippers, the members of the committee urged the formation of a fruit growers' union, and in February 1896 the Maricopa County Fruit Growers' Association came into being with Winfield Scott installed as interim president. In addition to being able to deal from strength with large produce brokers in the East and Midwest, Scott and his fellow incorporators planned to set up a wholesale shipping business and a farmers' market in order to eliminate the middleman as much as possible. The marketing and shipping of green fruit showed signs of coming of age in the Salt River Valley.

Scott also became increasingly involved in politics at all levels. Having modestly begun his career in 1894 as a precinct election inspector, he continued to serve in that capacity in both primary and general elections, and in the spring of 1896 he was elected as a delegate to a Republican county convention. Scott received an unpleasant lesson in political reality at that gathering, because he "insisted on honesty when it was an unwelcome and despised article." The politicians

The Howard Underhill home, situated near the northwest corner of the modern intersection of Scottsdale and Indian School Roads. Constructed in 1897 of adobe blocks and completely surrounded by a wide veranda, the Underhill home was a popular spot with early winter visitors to Scottsdale. (Mrs. Ruth M. Elliott, Phoenix, Arizona)

The tent home of the Reverend Judson A. Elliott and his family. The Reverend Elliott in familiar Prince Albert collar, his daughter Elsie, and Mrs. Elliott make up the trio in the left center portion of the photograph. This typical tent house stood on the Scottsdale townsite on what today has become the southeast corner of Scottsdale and Indian School Roads. (Mrs. Ruth M. Elliott, Phoenix, Arizona)

whose feathers he ruffled made certain he was not a delegate to the next convention. His work in the party and his stature in the community did not go unnoticed, however, and in the fall of 1896 he received the Maricopa County Republican nomination as one of four candidates for the Arizona House of Representatives. He had to decline the nomination, however, for his 1893 army furlough was still in effect, and the adjutant general ruled that as a member of the armed forces, he could not run for political office.

Chaplain Scott's greatest involvement in the valley was in the promotion of Scottsdale and the development of its nascent interests. He worked unceasingly to get the town started. Corresponding with friends and associates of a lifetime, he canvassed the East and Midwest for families who might be interested in moving west. He corresponded with families suggested to him or who had heard of his town and had written requesting information. The great majority of these families had one or more members with some respiratory ailment for which the desert was the prescribed cure. All Scott had to offer was clean air, soft water, fertile soil, and a helping hand. For some that was enough.

When Scott heard of someone in Phoenix who wanted to live out in the desert, he called on them to make a sales pitch. To choose the spartan, pioneer existence of living in Scottsdale over the amenities of civilization available in Phoenix took a hardy individual with a decided need to live in the desert. That need usually arose from health reasons or from a desire to lead a simpler, more wholesome life. Scott gradually found individuals with these persuasions and convinced them to join him.

George Blount, his wife Alza, and their three children were one family that chose the desert over the city. Leaving Illinois to come west for Mrs. Blount's health, they first settled in Phoenix with Alza Blount's brother, while George Blount found a position teaching in the Central School. After two moves toward the edge of the Phoenix settlement, the Blounts decided to move far into the desert for the cleanest, dryest air. Chaplain Scott heard of their decision and went to see them. As Blount's daughter Bertha recounts the story, her father became enthralled with Scott's plans and soon bought a forty-acre tract adjoining the southeast corner of the townsite. As the first family to move into the new neighborhood, the Blounts' arrival signaled the beginning of settlement in Scottsdale.

Other families had settled in the vicinity of Scott's ranch long before the Blounts came, but they had not come to live in Scottsdale. They have to be considered independent pioneers and not part of the original Scottsdale settlement. Once people began to settle in Scottsdale, however, they reached out to include these peripheral neighbors in the community. The Wilford Haydens from Missouri were one of the first families to be included. They had originally settled along the bottomlands of the Salt River near Phoenix, but the flood of 1891 devastated their farm, and they moved on to try again on a half section of land two miles southeast of Scott's ranch. The Haydens became an integral part of the Scottsdale community, and their six children helped the neighborhood reach the number of children required to form a school district.

Other families who lived in the neighborhood of Scott's ranch and who joined the Scottsdale community once it had been established were the Thomas U. Z. Kings, the Frank F. Tituses, and the John S. Taits. King had superintended Scott's ranch for a time after George Scott left in 1891 and lived two miles east of the chaplain. His son Oren was also included in the original count to form a school district. John Tait managed the Arizona Improvement Company's orchards about a mile and a half west of Scott, and Frank Titus built an impressive brick home and stables just a short distance south of the Haydens. They became part of the Scottsdale story, but only after others had written the prologue.

During the late fall of 1895 and the winter of 1896, families began to arrive. The Underhills from New York, the Ruhls from Kansas City, the Wards from Chicago, the Rosses from Minneapolis, and the Reverend Banks and his family from Toledo; they all came to settle in Scottsdale. Some chose to live on the townsite, others chose land nearby, and still others pitched tents on Scott's ranch. With the children from these families and the others already mentioned, there were soon enough prospective pupils in the neighborhood to form a school district. On June 30, 1896, Scott and some of the first settlers presented a petition to County School Superintendent C. W. Crouse, asking that a district be formed. On July 13, with the affirmative recommendation of the probate judge, the Maricopa County Board of Supervisors authorized the formation of School District Number Forty-eight "at Scotts-Dale." The little community had been officially recognized. Scott, John Tait, and Frank Titus were appointed by the community to the first school board.[3] To build a schoolhouse, these men requisitioned what little money there was available from the county school fund and went to the new citizens of Scottsdale for the rest. On a Saturday morning in mid-September, the men of Scottsdale assembled at the center of the townsite* and in the finest western tradition raised the one-room schoolhouse. While the men worked with hammer and nail, the women

---

*The school itself no longer stands, but the original site is located approximately ten yards east of the red brick schoolhouse on the Scottsdale Mall.

Original Scottsdale schoolhouse standing in the middle of the Scottsdale townsite. Using today's landmarks, it would be located about ten yards east of the Little Red Schoolhouse on the Scottsdale Mall. Camelback Mountain is visible in the left background and Mummy Mountain in the right background. Note also the ever-present Pima brush shed. (Mrs. May Vanderhoof Mathis, Scottsdale, Arizona)

prepared a picnic in the Scotts' shady grove. With the job complete, save for the framing of the windows and doors, everyone adjourned to Winfield Scott's to celebrate. His efforts had brought to fruition the Scottsdale idea. However small, the almost empty townsite, neatly marked off with little white stakes, was becoming a town.

The day following the raising of the schoolhouse was Sunday, and everyone gathered in the new building to organize a Sunday school. A service followed Sunday school, and three mandolins accompanied the singing of the old hymns. It is not difficult to imagine the sixteen-by-eighteen-foot room, set off by itself in the desert, echoing with the strains of "Amazing Grace," one of Scott's favorite hymns. For many years thereafter, Scottsdale held union services in the schoolhouse on Sunday morning. With several ministers living in the neighborhood, there was always someone available to preach the sermon, and the people could not ask for a better biblical scholar than Scott.

After the morning service in those early days George Blount hitched up his cart and with some of his neighbors rode out to the Pima Reservation to hold services in a brush shed. After the chief climbed to the roof of his roundhouse and called the people together, Blount preached through an interpreter, and his neighbors helped with the singing. Sunday evening the Scottsdale community gathered in the Blounts' sitting room for a prayer meeting. During the summer the meeting convened on the front porch, and the piano was rolled to the front door. In the words of Bertha Blount, those days were to be cherished for a lifetime. "The whole community gathered. There was little formality; all were well acquainted and the fellowship was intimate and fine."

In preaching to the Pimas, George Blount continued a work begun by Winfield Scott. From an early date, Scott's involvement in the affairs of the Salt River Valley included a friendly relationship with the Pimas. According to Elsie Elliott Severance, who knew Scott when she was a young girl and who listened to her parents speak of him often, Chaplain Scott went to the Pimas sometime after he purchased his section of land and asked the permission of the chief to settle there. His gesture was, of course, not legally necessary, but it showed both a sensitivity toward and an astute awareness of his Indian neighbors. In addition, Scott preached "the Jesus Way" to the Pimas when other commitments permitted and created a Christian cemetery for them. The Pimas, in turn, taught Scott and the early residents of Scottsdale how to build brush arbors to shade themselves from the summer sun. These crude structures of cottonwood limbs used as poles and cross-braces, and palo verde and mesquite limbs used as covering were a common sight in front of the tent homes of early Scottsdale. Even the schoolhouse had its own brush arbor. The Pimas also worked for Scott harvesting some of his crops, for which they were paid either in cash or on shares. For eight years Blount continued Scott's early mission to the Pimas. The Presbyterian church took over the mission officially in 1897, but for many years the people of Scottsdale continued Chaplain Scott's beginnings with their own selfless efforts.

In 1897 Scottsdale gained more of the trappings of a community and sharpened its sense of identity. The town held its first school board election in which twenty-nine votes were cast. Many of these votes came from women whom Helen Scott brought to the polls in her buggy from the outlying reaches of the district. Women had been able to vote in Arizona school elections since 1883, and Helen Scott was determined to see them exercise their franchise in Scottsdale school matters.

Since Winfield Scott held strong temperance views, it is not surprising that his community became a hotbed of temperance activity. He attracted people of similar persuasion, including Albert G. Utley. On the town lot reserved for the store and post office, Utley included a deed restriction prohibiting the sale of intoxicants. He further pledged to totally prohibit the sale of liquor on the townsite. Few wondered, then, at Scottsdale's vote for prohibition in May 1897 and the formation of the territory's first Anti-Saloon League in June. As Alza Blount phrased it for the *Phoenix Herald,* "It is the determination of the first settlers of Scottsdale never to let alcohol get a foothold in this part of

The first Scottsdale post office and general store opened by Scottsdale's first postmaster, J. L. Davis, in 1897. This building stood at what would become the southwest corner of Brown Avenue and Main Street. (Arizona Historical Society)

the valley. We are on the ground first and we do not propose to be caught napping."

Scottsdale officially received its United States Post Office in August, putting the town permanently on the map. The postmaster, J. L. Davis, also opened a general store, and Scottsdale residents no longer had to travel to Tempe or Phoenix for essentials. To accommodate winter visitors seeking the peace and quiet of the country, Scottsdale people began to add rooms to their homes or to pitch extra tents on their lots. In November Scott added two rooms to his new adobe home for just that purpose. The winter visitor industry in Scottsdale, a modern mainstay of the community's economy, can be traced to these early, simple beginnings. They could not compete with the newly opened Castle Hot Springs resort for the affluent winter visitors, but every winter the extra rooms in Scottsdale were full.

Christmas that year and in the years to come was a community celebration. To begin the festivities for their second holiday season together, the Scotts gave a dinner party on December 23. Some of the new residents and a sprinkling of the old gathered for a meal prepared almost entirely from the products of Scott's ranch. On Christmas Eve everyone gathered at the schoolhouse to await the arrival of Santa Claus. The school was decorated with pepper tree boughs and Christmas bells, and although Scottsdale would not have telephone service until 1909, a special "line" was installed to receive messages from Santa. Chaplain Scott was there to tell the Christmas story "as if it had happened yesterday," the Reverend Judson A. Elliott preached a sermon, and Professor Blount led the singing of the carols. Scott then slipped away to prepare for the arrival of Santa Claus.

All evening long, calls had been received relaying Santa's progress. He left his reindeer in Prescott and proceeded toward Phoenix with a team of broncos. Each step along the way, Glendale, Phoenix, the Crosscut Canal, brought another call and heightened excitement. Finally, bells outside signaled his arrival, and he was escorted into the schoolhouse to dispense a small gift to each child. Scott played the role with such zest that Elsie Elliott Severance remembers believing he was really Santa. His "twinkling blue eyes," salt-and-pepper beard, and a bit of a disguise were convincing enough to the children. Elsie remembers receiving a hand-embroidered handkerchief from Santa one year, while the boys received rubber balls. Another year the younger children each received a pencil while the older ones were given a pen and notebook. In those early simple days of Scottsdale's existence, sentiment truly counted for more than the gift.

On Christmas Day the Scotts shared a turkey dinner with the Elliotts, and everyone in the community was either guest or host for the

Winfield Scott's adobe home located on the northeast corner of the modern intersection of Scottsdale and Indian School Roads. Note the Pima brush shed on the left, the water well in the center, and the adobe cookhouse and hired hands' dining hall on the right. (Mrs. Ruth M. Elliott, Phoenix, Arizona)

Christmas feast. The sense of community was strong and growing. To conclude the Christmas celebration that year, the people of Scottsdale planned a surprise party for a young family in their midst. The Reverend C. J. Banks and his wife had come to Scottsdale the previous winter to try to regain his health. As he grew stronger, he was able to begin preaching again, and the community prevailed upon him to become their permanent pastor. For several months he had served admirably, and his congregation chose the Christmas season to show their appreciation. Three days after Christmas everyone assembled to give the Reverend Banks an old-fashioned "pounding." Each family brought a pound of some article–meat, flour, poultry, fruit–to his tent on Scott's ranch and caught the young couple completely by surprise. The beds, tables, and floor of the Bankses' tent were soon covered with packages, and after "an appropriate speech by Chaplain Scott," everyone adjourned to the Underhill home for an evening of games and conversation. This act of community thoughtfulness brought a fitting end to the Christmas season. If a schoolhouse, a post office, and an Anti-Saloon League defined Scottsdale's form, its strong sense of community enriched its substance.

For Scott, personally, 1897 was a year of new challenges and continuing commitments. From time to time he filled pulpits in Tempe and Phoenix, and he taught twenty-six students in his Scottsdale Bible class. With the passing months more newcomers came to live in his home or to tent on his ranch. Once again he received the appointment of chaplain in the Arizona militia. On his ranch he experimented with a new variety of apricot, which the *Herald* described as being quite large, smooth skinned, and exquisitely flavored. Having attained a reputation for excellence in fruit growing, Scott sold his table grape crop to a Phoenix dealer two months before the harvest. By early September there were twelve tons of raisins boxed in his shed, the product of his vineyard and that of Kansas newcomer William A. Telford. The bulk of the raisins came from Scott's vines, but more were expected from small growers, and it seems obvious that Scott had established a marketing cooperative in order to help the small growers in his neighborhood. By combining their grapes with Scott's they could command carload freight rates and could deal from strength when talking price with eastern buyers. Not all of Scott's challenges and commitments were as pleasant, however.

By this time Dr. Ford's orange orchard, under Scott's care, had died, and Ford rented his land to newcomers to grow broom corn. This failure must have been an embarrassment to Scott, especially since Ford's acreage had high visibility directly south of the townsite. In November Scott's peanut harvest amounted to only 3,500 pounds.

There could be several explanations for this significant drop, not the least of which was the drought that had fastened itself upon the valley during 1897.[4] The drought may also account for Scott plowing under five acres of vineyard in December to plant alfalfa. Alfalfa had always been a staple crop in the economy of the Salt River Valley, but as the livestock herds of the valley multiplied, especially the dairy herds, it became an increasingly important crop. Yielding five or six cuttings per year, it proved both prolific and profitable, and Scott always kept an eye open for profitable opportunities. Although needing a great deal of water to grow a luxuriant crop, alfalfa was also particularly resistant to drought, and this may have been his primary reason for planting it. As the drought continued into 1898, Scott prepared more acreage for alfalfa.

The fall of 1897 brightened for Scott, however, when his daughter Florence was accepted at the University of California at Berkeley. Florence had lived with her married sister Helen for two years while attending Alameda High School in Oakland, and now she entered the university's College of Chemistry as a premedical student. For a man who keenly believed in education, his daughter's accomplishment surely assuaged some of the season's problems.

During 1898 Scott's community involvement continued on many levels. On Arbor Day he purchased twenty-five ash trees so that each child in Scottsdale could plant a tree around the schoolhouse. He once again occupied the pulpit of the Tempe Baptist church until a new pastor was found and while there held a series of lectures for young people. Scott also served as foreman of the Maricopa County Grand Jury and worked as a member of the grand jury committee assigned to investigate the infamous Block 41.

Bounded by Madison, Jackson, Fifth, and Sixth Streets and located in approximately the southeast corner of the then Phoenix city limits,* Block 41 housed a notorious collection of brothels, saloons, and gaming rooms. It had been created in 1894 to contain prostitution in Phoenix within a defined reservation, but Scott and his associates found "the necessary evil" of Block 41 an iniquitous cancer on the community. Since it existed legally, the grand jury report could do little more than call for tighter control and regulation of the area. Specifically, the report recommended "that women of the district be prevented from appearing upon the street and in doorways in a dress calculated to advertise their immorality." Also recognizing that Block 41 would not have existed without the tacit support of the community,

---

*The initial city limits of Phoenix encompassed an area a mile long by a half mile wide with Harrison Street the southern boundary, Van Buren the northern, Seventh Avenue the western, and Seventh Street the eastern.

the committee, which included Samuel A. Dysart and J. M. Gregory, closed its report with an appeal to the community. "We believe that all good citizens should combine to formulate and encourage a public sentiment in our midst that will not permit the existence and continuance of such immoral tendencies."

The political heat generated by the grand jury report soon forced the city council to abolish Block 41, and the police were instructed to enforce an ordinance already on the books which outlawed prostitution throughout the city. By July 1 the ladies of the evening had vacated the area, but the victory proved to be a hollow one and somewhat ironic. Leaving behind them cards tacked to their old doorways indicating new addresses, the "nymphs du pave" scattered to all parts of the town, but most especially into the county where prostitution remained a legal endeavor.

In the fall of 1898 Scott once again took an active role in Republican politics, both "toiling in the trenches" and sitting in the party's councils. At the county convention, Scott nominated Marcus W. Messinger, cashier of the Valley Bank, as candidate for county treasurer and had the additional honor of nominating Captain James H. McClintock of the Rough Riders as Republican candidate to the upper house of the territorial legislature. Chaplain Scott's patriotic nominating speech roused the audience to such an extent that, when Edwin Gill followed and asked the delegates to unanimously accept the nomination by standing, they rose and roared their approval.

Captain McClintock was, at that time, in the hospital at Fort Wadsworth on Staten Island recovering from a serious leg wound received in Cuba, and Scott read a telegram from the captain indicating he would run if called upon to do so. The Republican party was proud of its members who had served with the Rough Riders in the Spanish-American War, and McClintock's nomination was a popular one. Scott's personal honor came later when his name, along with those of J. W. Benham, Sam Brown, and B. T. Gillette, was placed in nomination as candidate for the territorial house of representatives. The nomination was approved by acclamation. Having been officially retired from the service in March, Scott accepted. In the Scott family tradition, the chaplain was in harness and about to begin a vigorous and spirited campaign.

CHAPTER X

New Challenges and Old Missions

The Republican territorial convention was held September 20 in Prescott, and Lieutenant Colonel Alexander O. Brodie, Theodore Roosevelt's successor as commanding officer of the Rough Riders, was nominated as the Republican candidate for delegate to Congress. As a territory, Arizona had no senators or congressmen, and the delegate to Congress was the territory's voice on Capitol Hill. Arizona was still in the midst of a severe drought, and the need for a comprehensive water storage project was felt more acutely than ever before. Arizona's delegate to Congress would play an important role in advocating Arizona's interests to the next session of Congress. He would be expected to lobby strenuously and effectively for statehood and for the right of Arizona's farmers to bond their land in order to build reservoirs. Without statehood, private capital from outside sources was reluctant to invest in Arizona irrigation projects, and without bonding authority, the farmers of Arizona could not do it themselves. Naturally, the Republicans felt that a Republican delegate to Congress would be more effective in presenting Arizona's case, and the election of Brodie took priority. Placing his own campaign second, Scott campaigned for Brodie not only in Maricopa County but in Graham County as well.

The campaign was joined in earnest in late September, and political meetings and rallies were held almost every day except Sunday. On October 7 the rally was held in Mesa. A large platform had been erected near the Barnett Building, and wire had been strung for electric lights. Several hundred people attended, occupying benches set up for the occasion. Cowboys, ranchers, and townspeople formed a large semicircle behind the benches, and an assemblage of carriages and buggies filled with interested onlookers formed the outer perimeter. As was usually the case, Scott was the last speaker on the program, because he had the ability to end a program on a high note. The rally in Mesa was no exception. Scott spoke for twenty minutes and was frequently interrupted by applause. Several evenings later, Scott spoke at the formation of a Republican club in the Cartwright district, and the *Arizona Republican* reported that the chaplain's oratory had surpassed his previous efforts. The next evening he was cheered at a meeting in the Orme district northwest of Phoenix as he argued for the election of the Republican county ticket. While Scott gave his utmost for the party, the two Republican papers, the *Phoenix Herald* and the *Arizona Republican,* campaigned for the chaplain.

With the exception of Colonel Brodie, who led the Republican ticket, Scott received the most vocal praise and extensive coverage in the Republican press. In addition to quoting his speeches and recording his activities, the papers, as they did for all candidates, editorialized on his ability, character, and energy. Said the *Herald,* "He has been one of the leading factors in the settlement of the great west in years gone by as a commissioner of immigration in Kansas." Added the *Republican,* "As a citizen of the valley he has always labored to build up its resources, and few men have done more toward bringing about diversified ranching in the valley." As the supreme accolade for a Republican candidate in that year of 1898, the *Republican* inserted these two lines on its editorial page on election eve, "Chaplain Scott, like Teddy Roosevelt, is a born fighter. He will fight any interests which are antagonistic to the welfare of Arizona." Readily acknowledging that these were newspapers with a strong Republican orientation backing Republican candidates for public office, it was nevertheless true that the praise showered upon Scott far surpassed that accorded the other Republican county candidates. His career had been a testament to man's courage, energy, and conviction, and it made good copy. The *Republican* went so far as to print long accounts of Scott's Civil War experiences in its news columns. By highlighting his remarkable career, the newspaper was helping further the campaigns of the other Republican candidates on the ticket with Scott.

In late October Chaplain Scott toured Graham County for Colonel Brodie. He spoke of the drought and the need for water storage projects. Statehood was vital to any successful program of reservoir construction, and Colonel Brodie was the man to help win statehood for Arizona. At Willcox, Pima, Thatcher, and Safford, Scott spoke on behalf of Brodie and, as a farmer, spoke to the farmers in their own language. At Safford he not only occupied the political platform but the

pulpit of the local church as well. On the political platform he compli-
mented the farmers and ranchers of the Gila Valley on their increasing
productivity and on their fine system of irrigation canals. In his opinion
the Gila Valley had great potential, and he advised his fellow agricul-
turists to maintain local control of their canals. Scott proposed that
Colonel Brodie was the man to help them and the territory realize the
greatest potential and, in the archetypal political endorsement, char-
acterized him as a friend of the miner, rancher, and workingman. Although Scott campaigned vigorously for Brodie, his efforts would not
overcome the traditional Democrat majority in the county.

Candidate Scott returned to Phoenix for the close of the campaign
where the Republicans staged two meetings on the Saturday evening
preceding election day. The first was held in O'Neill Hall and was
closely followed by one at the old opera house. Scott spoke at both
meetings and ended the evening as the last speaker at the opera house.
He began from personal experience and closed with a call for Brodie's
election:

> I want to talk for my ranch and for every ranch in Arizona. . . . Our
> vineyards and orchards are crying for water. Unless we can get more
> water many of our ranches must go to waste. I was compelled to grub out
> eighty acres of orchard at my ranch because there was not sufficient
> water to allow them to flourish. We are holding on, waiting and hoping
> that we may yet be able to save our homes. . . . Reservoirs will not be
> built until Arizona becomes a state. The government will not help us and
> won't until we are a state with representation in Congress and the Sen-
> ate. . . . Mr. Wilson, the Democratic candidate for delegate to Congress,
> admits in his speeches that he can do nothing for us. He says he cannot
> secure statehood. Let the people of Arizona take him at his word and give
> their support to a man who believes he can attain this great desire of the
> people. Col. Brodie says he can get statehood and the people have
> confidence in his ability to accomplish what he sets out to do. He has
> never failed in the past and he will not fail now.

On Monday evening the Republicans held rallies in Phoenix,
Mesa, and Tempe. Scott was dispatched with Judge Crouse to Mesa to
ring down the curtain on the campaign. It had been a grueling, nonstop
canvass, but he had managed to fulfill his other duties. He preached
every Sunday, presided at a funeral in Tempe, and addressed the Arizona Baptist Association's annual meeting. In the interim, he tried to
save his remaining acres of fruit trees as the drought in the Salt River
Valley continued.

On November 8 Winfield Scott won election to the territorial
house of representatives. Of the eight candidates Scott received the
third highest vote total, being surpassed by young Republican J. W.

Benham and Mesa Democrat Charles Peterson. Sam Brown, a Tempe Republican, was the fourth candidate elected. The Republicans had done well in Maricopa County, capturing eight of ten county offices. They also gave Brodie a seventy-vote majority in the race for delegate to Congress, but it was not enough to overcome Democrat majorities in other counties, and Colonel John F. Wilson was elected. James McClintock was not released from the hospital in time to campaign in his bid for a council seat and lost to Aaron Goldberg by 70 votes out of 4,344 cast. Overall, it was a bleak campaign for the Rough Riders. After being showered with an enthusiastic outpouring of public affection, not one of the six Rough Rider veterans was elected to office in Arizona. Softening Republican disappointment at this turn of events was their showing in Maricopa County. In 1896 they had gathered only 32 percent of the vote, but in this election they captured 51 percent. These larger political considerations counted for little in Scottsdale, where the people were jubilant over the election of their Chaplain Scott. Lemonade toasts, speeches, and a picnic celebration were the order of the day. It was a proud moment for the little town.

With the election behind them, the people of the valley again focused their attention on the ominous specter of drought. In mid-December territorial Senator-elect Aaron Goldberg called a meeting of Salt River Valley farmers, ranchers, and businessmen to discuss plans for developing a water storage system for the valley. Along with W. J. Murphy and Lincoln Fowler, Scott addressed the meeting. His stature as an innovative and hardworking farmer and his vigorous campaigning on the water storage issue had earned him a voice. A committee was formed to advance the water storage project and to keep it before the public. Governor Nathan Oakes Murphy was to chair the committee, and, among other interested farmers, ranchers, and businessmen, Fowler, Goldberg, and Scott were appointed to assist him. Chaplain Scott now rented his ranch for the winter and prepared to live in Phoenix during the coming legislative session. The long buggy ride back and forth to the ranch every day would have taken too much time and energy, two highly prized commodities during the coming term.

On January 16, 1899, the House of Representatives of the Twentieth Legislative Assembly of the Territory of Arizona was sworn in by Chief Justice Webster Street of the Arizona Supreme Court.* The only substantive business that day entailed the election of the Speaker of the House, and Chaplain Scott had the honor of receiving his party's nomination. Henry F. Ashurst, Democratic representative from Coconino

---

*Until the capitol was completed in 1901, the legislature met in second floor chambers in the Phoenix City Hall.

Phoenix City Hall, located on the block bounded by First and Second Streets, Washington and Jefferson. Here Winfield Scott first addressed the people of Phoenix in 1888, and here he served in the territorial legislature in 1899. Judging from the size of the trees and the fact that B. Heyman Furniture Company does not yet occupy the Anderson Block, shown here in the right background, this photograph was probably taken at about the time of Scott's first Phoenix speech. (Historical Collection of Herb and Dorothy McLaughlin, Phoenix, Arizona)

County and future United States senator from Arizona, received his party's nomination. As there were thirteen Democrats and eleven Republicans in the lower house, Ashurst was elected by two votes. On that first day of the legislative session, Scott also attended a meeting of Governor Murphy's water storage committee.

The only business on the committee's agenda consisted of two requests from Scott concerning possible water storage legislation. First, he asked that the group draft a bill on water storage and, second, that the committee inform the press of its interest in obtaining public opinion on the subject. The proposal that was finally adopted and which Scott incorporated in his House Bill 120, called for the creation of irrigation districts similar to those employed in the Wright Reclamation Act of California. By the time Scott's bill passed the lower house and was reported out of committee in the upper house, it was the last day of the session, and no action was taken. Winfield Scott would be a progressive thorn in the side of a conservative house and would pursue an independent course on matters of principle. In this instance, however, on a matter of grave concern to everyone, he worked well with the water storage committee and within the legislature to try to effect a solution.

In all, Chaplain Scott introduced sixteen bills before the legislature, four of which became law. These provided for the revision of the laws of Arizona Territory, an amendment to the school laws of Arizona to allow children living in one district to go to school in another, the purchase of a case to house the Rough Riders' battle flag, and a bill for the relief of Charles D. Poston, "the father of Arizona." These bills passed the Democrat-controlled legislature, because they were innocuous and nonpartisan. His bills with any substance or partisan hue were either defeated or "postponed so indefinitely . . . they wouldn't be in sight on the judgement day." They were simply too liberal for the conservative political climate which held sway in the legislature. Winfield Scott's political philosophy embraced the progressive movement then gaining currency in the land, and his defeated bills reflected the tenets of that movement. He introduced bills for the prevention of cruelty to animals, for the taxation of mines, and for direct legislation by the people of Arizona. He drafted legislation to allow municipal home rule for Arizona cities and unincorporated towns, and two of his favorite bills called for the Sunday closing of saloons and a prohibition on gambling. All these measures were progressive in outlook, especially the ones calling for municipal home rule and direct legislation; these clearly mirrored the reform belief in "the efficacy of democracy."[1] In a broad sense they also reflected the tenets of the social gospel. For Scott, and for many doctrinally liberal clergymen, the espousal of these beliefs was a natural outgrowth of the social gospel.

Thwarted at every turn in his attempts at progressive legislation, Scott did not concede without a fight. His effort to get a hearing for his antigambling bill began a session-long confrontation with Democratic representative W. S. Adams of Jerome. A motion to table the bill after it was first read drew a strong protest from Scott who asserted that many good citizens supported the measure. Adams responded that the good citizens of his constituency did not support the measure, and the battle lines were drawn.

Once the bill was referred to the committee on education, Adams attempted to get it transferred to the committee on territorial affairs of which he was a member. He failed. At the same time, in support of his bill, Scott introduced a petition with seven hundred signatures. The petition failed to impress Scott's legislative brethren, and when the antigambling bill came up again, they recommended that it be indefinitely postponed. Scott refused to be put off and moved to make the bill a special order for March 3. Adams rejoined with another motion to indefinitely postpone, but Scott would have none of it. He gained the floor once again and proposed to speak for three hours in order to get his bill its due consideration. He began a well-prepared and fiery denunciation of gambling, as his political opponents slipped quietly from the chamber. Adams and his cohorts were in no mood to listen to Scott's oratory, especially since it was five in the afternoon. Someone asked that the missing members be returned to their seats, and the sergeant-at-arms was sent to retrieve them. Returning to the house floor, he reported that he had found the errant members, but they refused to return. Speaker Ashurst issued an ultimatum; return immediately or be barred from the floor until proper apologies were tendered. The missing members returned with great haste. A motion to kill debate was defeated, and Scott had won the day. Adams and his cohorts realized they were stymied and decided to compromise. If Scott would save his speech, the bill would be taken up as a special order on March 3. The procedural battle had been won.

The war was lost, however, when the bill came up for consideration March 3. Scott, inexplicably, lost his political senses that day and with scathing contempt introduced a resolution asking that two hundred copies of certain sections of the Arizona penal law be printed and distributed among house members and lobbyists "so that the ability to sin ignorantly would be avoided." The sections to be printed dealt with bribery of members of the legislature. Adams was furious and objected to the reading of the resolution, declaring it an insult to every member of the house. In the skirmishing that followed, the resolution was tabled. It is doubtful that this righteous indignation changed the course of events, but the outburst may have changed the margin of defeat. When the antigambling bill came up for consideration, it was defeated seventeen to five.

Scott and Adams had one final confrontation toward the end of the session. With the Speaker of the House away on business, the Democrat majority joined their Republican counterparts to make Scott speaker pro tem for an evening session. Scott, in a reciprocal goodwill gesture, relaxed the no-smoking ban in the house which he had pushed through early in the session. During the evening, Adams rose to request the reading of an upper house bill, and Scott indicated a majority vote was needed to have the bill read for information. In a voice that brought the members of the upper house running to the lower house lobby, Adams declared Scott's decision "the most outrageous ruling since God Almighty made creation." Scott ordered Adams arrested, to which the representative from Jerome shouted, "Take me down! Put me in Jail! I won't be bulldozed. I want my rights and I'm going to have them." During this display of histrionics, Scott regained his composure and called for a vote on the motion to read the bill. It failed, but Adams continued the bombast and did most of the bulldozing, until the house reconsidered and let him have his reading. This unfortunate scene concluded Scott's tenure in the chair, and the session-long confrontation came to an end.

There was one pleasant respite for Scott during the political wars of the Twentieth Legislative Assembly. He was assigned to the committee charged with investigating the condition of the territorial university in Tucson. Education played an important role in Winfield Scott's life, and he championed its cause at every turn. This assignment allowed him to tour the University of Arizona and inspect its workings. He and his fellow committee members approved of what they saw and produced a highly favorable report. While Scott was at the university, he was invited to speak to the assembled student body. This would not be his last opportunity to address the students, however, for several years later he would return to Tucson as a member of the board of regents and chancellor of the university.

In mid-March the legislature adjourned, and Scott returned to his ranch and resumed his full schedule. He attended the annual convention of the Arizona Baptist Association in Phoenix, where he preached the missionary sermon. At this gathering Scott shared the limelight with his wife, who presided over the meeting of the Women's Missionary Society. Helen Scott took an active role in both church and community affairs, and she often shared center stage with her husband.

With the convention barely over, Scott ran for a seat on the board of the Phoenix Union High School district, which at that time included Scottsdale. During the campaign, the supporters of his opponent claimed that he favored the separation of the high school from the Phoenix grade schools of the district. It was an extremely unpopular position and one that he vehemently denied taking. He circulated handbills to that effect, but the damage had been done, and he lost the election by a two-to-one margin.

In early May the apricot harvest began, and Scott busied himself in the orchard. He also continued his touring ministry, receiving invitations to preach in Mesa and to participate in the Memorial Day services in Phoenix. The sixty-two-year-old Scott gave little evidence that he had "retired" six years previously.

During the spring Scott made plans to spend the summer in Prescott. The secretary of war granted him permission to occupy officer's quarters at Fort Whipple, and he arrived in Prescott in mid-June to make the necessary living arrangements. On this first of many trips to the Yavapai County seat, he also preached in the Baptist church. By the time he returned to Scottsdale to escort his wife to their summer residence, he had agreed to supply the pulpit for the summer. The Prescott *Journal-Miner* gave Scott a heady introduction to the town, describing his long career in some detail and calling him a "wide-awake progressive citizen and magnetic public speaker." Scott soon gave everyone a chance to decide for themselves, when he issued an invitation to the public to attend patriotic services on the Sunday following the Fourth of July. He wasted little time in initiating efforts to build up his new congregation.

Winfield Scott had an inveterate booster's spirit, and before long he was singing the praises of his summer home. In early August the *Phoenix Herald* received a letter from Scott promoting Prescott as a summer resort. With all the aplomb of a veteran world traveler, he stated that based on his nine years' experience in California, Prescott's summer climate was superior. The Prescott papers, naturally, thrived on this fare, and Scott received good press coverage while he lived there. On his return from a trip to Scottsdale for the grape harvest, Scott presented boxes of his grapes to both Prescott papers. Being an astute businessman, as well as an intelligent booster, he recognized the opportunity to expand into a new market with some free advertising. Winfield Scott worked tirelessly for the interests he championed, whether they were his own, a town's, or a church's, and much to his credit, everyone around him usually benefited from his efforts.

Helen Scott not only followed her own career in church and community affairs, she also assisted her husband's career whenever the opportunity arose. Scott made several trips to his ranch that summer,

Prescott, Arizona Territory, as viewed from the southwest. Note the Yavapai County Courthouse in the center of the photograph. Whiskey Row along Montezuma Street is situated just west of the courthouse. It is believed this photograph was taken at about the time of Scott's fifteen month stay in Prescott. (National Archives Photograph, Barry Goldwater Collection, Arizona Historical Foundation)

and when he had to leave unexpectedly, Helen filled the pulpit on Sunday evening. She spoke well, kept her audience interested, and according to the *Journal-Miner*, her address "contained . . . evidences of a scholarly mind and a warm sympathetic heart." She also helped her husband in more traditional ways, inviting the ladies' aid of the church out to Fort Whipple, where the refreshments included fresh fruit from her husband's ranch. With the passing years, Helen Scott's aversion to summer in the Salt River Valley had grown increasingly strong. This summer's trip to Prescott was probably undertaken primarily for her benefit, and she responded with yeoman service in support of her husband. In the years to come, she would spend every summer in California.

In late September the Prescott Baptist church asked Winfield Scott to become their pastor. The church existed under the auspices of the Home Mission Society of New York, and the officers of the society, all of whom were personal friends of Scott, also urged him to take charge of their mission church. Putting aside his political interest, Scott agreed to become pastor for one year. He rented his ranch in Scottsdale once again, donned his dusty missionary hat and went to work. Of his decision the *Journal-Miner* offered this appraisal, "His coming assures permanency and success to the Baptist cause in Prescott. . . . We congratulate the church on its good fortune."

For the next six months Chaplain Scott worked with youthful intensity to build and strengthen his congregation. His seventeen years of missionary experience served him well, as he sought ways to bring people into the church. In keeping with his long-held belief in the importance of music, Scott organized a new choir. He also organized a Baptist Young People's Union with eighteen members and a great deal of enthusiasm. Coupled with his interesting sermons and lectures, these new measures proved effective. Each Sunday found new students in Sunday school and new faces in the congregation. As he had done in Denver, Scott invited evangelists to preach in his church, and in March he inaugurated a series of revival meetings which moved Prescott as nothing had for years.

On one of his frequent, short trips to the Salt River Valley, Scott witnessed the great success enjoyed by the Reverend W. A. Pavy in his series of revival meetings in Phoenix, Tempe, and Mesa. Scott invited the Indiana evangelist to come to Prescott when his valley tour was complete, and Pavy accepted. Renowned as a speaker and a singer, Pavy had worked with the famous evangelist Dwight L. Moody, and his coming to Prescott stirred great interest. Scott spared no personal effort to insure the success of these meetings, and he enlisted the aid of his friend, the Reverend Judson A. Elliott, as well. Elliott came up from Scottsdale and together with Scott canvassed the town, extending personal invitations to everyone they contacted to come to the meetings. Pavy arrived to begin the services on a Sunday, and they continued every night of the week for the next seventeen days. At the services each night, people came forward to give testimony and to enlist in canvassing the town, and after the first week, the *Journal-Miner* said of Pavy, "No evangelist has ever held meetings in Prescott who is his equal." As the word of Pavy's preaching and singing spread, the little church became filled to overflowing, and people had to be turned away at the door. Minnie Elliott soon arrived from Scottsdale to assist in the services and to help with the canvassing, and Chaplain Scott urged all Christians "to come pray and unite in helping save men."

During the second week of the revival, it was decided to hold street meetings to reach those individuals who were not coming to the services. The first evening of these outdoor meetings, the members of the congregation and the newly won Christian workers assembled near the corner of Gurley and Montezuma Streets, within shouting distance of the saloons and gambling halls of fabled "Whiskey Row." Two to three hundred people soon gathered, many of them the denizens of "Whiskey Row," and to begin the meeting, the congregation sang "Throw Out the Life Line" with many joining in on the chorus. The Reverend Pavy then explained that he had come to give the men of the town a second invitation to come to the services. Chaplain Scott offered a prayer and gave a short address, and talks followed by Minnie Elliott and the Reverend Pavy. All were accorded a respectful hearing, and when the meeting adjourned to the church, a great many in the crowd followed along. For the next eight evenings, "all classes of citizens" attended the street meetings that were held by the lights left burning in the display windows of Joseph W. Wilson's clothing store. The two and a half weeks of church services, street meetings, and daily canvassing paid handsome dividends, and for many weeks thereafter Scott baptized new members of the Baptist church. The efforts of W. A. Pavy and the Judson A. Elliotts had helped Winfield Scott to build and strengthen his congregation.

While Scott worked to further the Baptist cause in Prescott, he also requested the adjutant general of the United States to elevate him from the retired list of chaplains to active duty in the Philippines. A year and a half earlier, he had written the war department requesting a physical examination and elevation to active duty. The sinking of the battleship *Maine* in Havana harbor stirred the old soldier's patriotism, and he wanted to serve if war broke out. The day he mailed his request for a physical examination, he received his official retirement notice. Instead of serving in the Spanish-American War, he bought revenue stamps and served in the territorial legislature. In mid-November 1899, however, with his son-in-law serving with the occupation forces in the Philippines, with the Filipino insurrection continuing, and with chaplains objecting to service on those Pacific islands, Scott tried once more to serve his country. He solicited the assistance of Governor N. O. Murphy, who wrote President McKinley in support of his application. He also wrote his own letters, indicating in one that his right leg was much improved and stating, "I feel sure that I could do duty, in the field or in the hospitals. My heart is in this war and I should like to be with the army at the front where I believe efficient service can be rendered." In another letter he called his health "superb" and closed by saying, "As an old soldier I would like to close my military career at the front and while doing duty, I feel sure that my experience as officer in the line, and chaplain, fits me as well as if not better, to do effective service during the war than any new man who could be appointed." Scott soon received word that a special act of Congress was necessary to activate him from the retired list, and he did not press for further action. By today's standards, his actions may be viewed as chauvinistic, but Winfield Scott was a patriot of the old school, who believed that "every man who can, should stand by the government, and be ready to follow and defend the flag."

Chaplain Scott used the revival meetings of March and the baptism of new members as points of departure and continued his efforts to further the Baptist cause in Prescott. He called upon the Christian workers who had assisted in the revivals to continue their spiritual work for the church. He organized a junior B.Y.P.U. with twenty members and planned a literary and musical evening similar to the ones held in Leavenworth. Scott initiated a new era of prosperity for the Prescott Baptist church and helped its members find a spirit of enthusiasm and purpose.

In April Scott journeyed to Mesa to attend the Arizona Baptist Association convention that was held during the Easter weekend. While he preached the Easter sermon for the convention, Helen Scott conducted Easter services in Prescott. There were times when Scott could not have fulfilled his myriad commitments without the support of his wife. In May, as department chaplain of the G.A.R., he attended the annual encampment in Jerome. In June he returned to Scottsdale to attend a meeting of the Scottsdale school board of which he was still a member. At the meeting he offered to buy a flagpole for the schoolhouse to be erected for the Fourth of July celebration, and although he would not be there, he offered his grove for the community celebration. His offers were accepted. In early September Scott's Prescott pastorate came to an end, and he returned to the valley in time to be elected delegate to the Republican county convention. The past two years had been full of new challenges and old missions, but the time had come for Scott to return home, at least for a while.

CHAPTER XI

In Perpetual Motion

In the months following his return to the valley, the pattern of Winfield Scott's life revolved around his community. He was elected superintendent of the Scottsdale Sunday school, he preached an occasional sermon in the schoolhouse, and he conducted the Thanksgiving Day service for the first time in several years. The Saturday before Christmas, Scott and his wife visited the frame cottages, adobe homes, and tents in the neighborhood, delivering Christmas boxes filled with oranges and grapefruit from their ranch. In his own way, Scott tried to make everyone feel that they belonged, and to a large extent, he succeeded. There were those who did not perceive his goodwill, however, and who resented the time he spent away from Scottsdale. These feelings must be acknowledged and given their due consideration, but it is difficult to imagine that those who felt a certain disaffection would begrudge or deny Scott's thoughtfulness that Christmas season to old friend and winter visitor alike.

During the winter of 1900–1901 more winter visitors came to Scottsdale than ever before, but even with this influx of newcomers, the village probably had a population of less than two hundred. By comparison, Phoenix and the adjoining subdivisions probably had a winter population of fifteen thousand. Some of the winter residents in Scottsdale brought their own tents that season and camped in the desert, taking their meals with nearby families who catered to table boarders. The wife of a Stanford University professor and a respected minister from the Midwest each chose to camp in the desert, while two sisters from Cornell University stayed with the Scotts, and a Stanford student boarded with the Underhills. Since Winfield Scott attracted people to

Scottsdale with backgrounds and interests similar to his own, the village gained the reputation of being an educated, Christian community. The people who came for the winter often came there for that reason and by their coming, enhanced the reputation.

The incidents of Scott's life during 1901 chronicle a year like many others he had spent and would spend in the valley. He preached in Phoenix and conducted the Memorial Day service in Tempe. At the dedication of the new territorial capitol building in Phoenix, he was invited, along with a small group of prominent Phoenicians, to share the platform with the governor, members of the legislature, and justices of the supreme court. As always, he attended the annual Baptist convention. Once again, Mother Nature proved him an astute judge of location when his apricots survived a late winter frost that killed the apricots in neighboring groves. The second year of the new century went by routinely for Scott until in early May a man known as "Popcorn John" upset the pattern.

The people of Phoenix called John Rubenstein "Popcorn John," because he sold popcorn on the courthouse plaza. He also carried the mail to Scottsdale, and his routine included having his lunch on Chaplain Scott's property before returning to Phoenix. One day after lunch he came through Scott's yard in his mail wagon, found his way blocked, and became agitated. Luckily, Scott was not in the yard. Immobilized on a cot because of a recently broken leg, Scott had been supervising the stacking of hay in a shed, but when his workers left to get more hay, they carried him into his home. As the workers returned to the front yard from the fields, their wagon had blocked Rubenstein's path. With no warning, and only a few irrational words to explain his actions, the mail carrier shot two of the field hands, Peter Johnson and Amos Nigh, to death. Rubenstein's motive for the killings is unclear, and the *Arizona Republican* simply stated that he was "undoubtedly crazy." In any event, he was apprehended on his way back to Phoenix, brought to trial, convicted, and sentenced to the territorial prison at Yuma. The significance of the tragedy, however, lies in the immediate aftermath of the shootings, for Peter Johnson was a Pima. Scott had himself lifted into a buggy and, with the assistance of Judson Elliott, drove out to the Pima village to inform the chief of the murder and to assure him that none of the Scottsdale people had committed the crime. The goodwill and trust of the Pimas was important to Scott and the community.

Shortly after the funerals, which were held in Scott's front yard, the chaplain began to move about in his buggy to attend to the working of his ranch. By late May he had begun again to accept invitations to preach. Helen Scott spent the summer in California, and in late August

View looking east, on what today is Indian School Road, toward Scottsdale, ca. 1900. The tall cottonwood tree in the center of the photograph was located on Winfield Scott's ranch on the northeast corner of the present-day intersection of Indian School and Scottsdale Roads. The Scottsdale townsite occupies the center and right background. (Barry Goldwater Collection, Arizona Historical Foundation)

Scott joined his family on the coast. While there he received notice that the board of education had appointed him to fill a vacancy on the Board of Visitors to the Normal School of Arizona at Tempe, today's Arizona State University. Composed of three prominent citizens, the board of visitors had been created to promote the cause of the normal school, and it issued a yearly report based on a personal inspection of the school. The board of education, the normal school's governing board, then used this report when dealing with the legislature for appropriations. Having served on the education committee of the territorial house of representatives and being an enthusiastic supporter of education, Scott proved to be an astute selection. For more than a year Winfield Scott had confined his activities in an area close to home, almost as if to gain strength from contact with his land and his community. The next few years, however, would reveal a much different pattern.

The spring of 1902 brought new directions and challenges to the Scotts. Helen Scott received important recognition with her election to the presidency of the Arizona Baptist Association, and in mid-April she presided over that group's annual convention. During the convention proceedings, the association's mission board called on Chaplain Scott to employ his church-building talents in southeastern Arizona, and in late April he journeyed to Douglas and Naco along the Mexican border.

In the fall of 1900 James S. Douglas and a group of associates had formed the International Land and Improvement Company to lay out a townsite, sell lots, and build and operate the utilities necessary for the town's development. James S. Douglas named the town in honor of his father, James Douglas, Jr., and the company began selling lots a few months later. With the certain establishment of two smelters nearby, the population of Douglas grew from approximately five hundred in 1901 to two thousand in May 1902.[1]

The Copper Queen Consolidated Mining Company, the largest of Phelps, Dodge and Company's properties in Arizona, planned to build one of the smelters near Douglas, and it had always been the policy of the parent company to help provide not only the essentials but also the amenities for its workers. James Douglas, Jr., president of the Copper Queen, saw that this policy was carried out,[2] and when Winfield Scott arrived to organize a congregation, secure a building lot, and raise funds to build a church, he had the active support of both the Copper Queen and "Professor" Douglas.

A similar situation prevailed in Naco. Colonel William C. Greene, founder of the Cananea Consolidated Copper Company, had a vested interest in Naco and supported Scott's efforts there. For several years

Naco had been the supply depot for Colonel Greene's copper mines in Cananea, Sonora, Mexico, and the shipping point for his copper ore to American smelters. In January 1902 he inaugurated service on his forty-five-mile railroad, the Cananea, Yaqui River and Pacific, between his copper mines in Cananea and the railhead in Naco.[3] It seems clear from Colonel Greene's support of Scott's work that he wanted to upgrade the community for the benefit of his workers living there. Perhaps the only difficult part of Scott's assignment centered in organizing congregations, for considering his sources of support, the selection of building lots and the raising of funds probably presented no major problem. Scott's experience still counted for a great deal, however, and he completed both assignments in six weeks. Helen Scott stepped in beside her husband in this venture also, when she personally donated the organ for the Douglas church. When Chaplain Scott left southeastern Arizona in early June, the Naco church was under construction and work on the Douglas church about to begin.

During his six-week stay in Douglas and Naco, Scott took the opportunity to visit Colonel Greene's mines in Cananea. He had long been interested in mining, but it is possible this trip was undertaken for more than just casual inspection. In the months to come he would become involved in two mining ventures, one of which was located southwest of Cananea. While in Mexico, Scott stayed with the superintendent of the company's supply department, C. J. Jaques, who as a boy had been a member of Scott's Sunday school in Reno. Even for a man whose career spanned half a continent, it is still surprising that Scott should meet an old friend in such a remote part of the world.

Returning to the valley from his border sojourn, Scott made preparations to be away from his ranch for the summer. Helen Scott left for California in mid-June, and he joined her in early July. Minnie Scott Albright and her husband were returning home from the Philippines, and the whole Scott family would be together for the first time in many years. Helen Scott Flint opened her Oakland home for the gathering of the clan, and Florence Scott came down from St. Helen's Hall, a women's college in Portland, Oregon, where she had been teaching science. After her graduation from the University of California with high honors in chemistry, the university recommended Florence to St. Helen's when that school wrote requesting a science teacher. Now her trip to Oakland for the reunion served a dual purpose; she had been hired to teach physics, mathematics, and chemistry in an Oakland area high school in the fall. Leaving his four girls to bring one another up to date, Winfield Scott began an extended business trip east in connection with his new mining ventures.

Scott had once again joined his Baptist brethren in a mining venture or, more correctly, two ventures. With the Reverend Judson A. Elliott and John T. Cave, Scott organized the Coast Line Copper Company to engage in copper mining in Mexico. The company was capitalized at $5 million, and the annual meeting was to be held in Nogales, Arizona. At this same time the Reverend George H. Brewer and Dr. John Wix Thomas, a deacon of the First Baptist Church of Phoenix, incorporated the Socorro Gold Mining Company to engage in gold mining in New Mexico. This company was capitalized at $500,000, and its annual meeting was scheduled for Albuquerque, New Mexico. Judson Elliott and Winfield Scott became charter members of the Socorro Company's board of directors, and Scott was elected the company's president. With these two new ventures to promote, Scott toured the country, or as Alza Blount put it, "Chaplain Scott continues to wander up and down the earth." He visited Colorado, New Mexico, Kansas, Missouri, Illinois, and many points east. He renewed acquaintances of a lifetime, and he undoubtedly invited more than a few to invest in his new ventures. He also filled a few pulpits along the way, including his old church in Denver, and spent some time in the Pacific Garden Mission in Chicago assisting in the church's work there.

Upon his return to Scottsdale in October, Scott received the news that Governor Alexander O. Brodie had appointed him to the Board of Regents of the University of Arizona. In the election of 1898 Scott had assisted Brodie's campaign for delegate to Congress, and now that Brodie had been appointed governor by President Theodore Roosevelt, he was most likely repaying a political debt. Given Scott's educational background, his continuing interest in the cause of education, and his knowledge of Arizona's institutions of higher learning gained through his legislative and board of visitors experience, the appointment was a good one.

Before traveling to Tucson in early November for a board of regents' meeting, Chaplain Scott took the opportunity to preach in the Scottsdale schoolhouse. In making the announcements that morning, Scott revealed again his position in the progressive mainstream. Remarking on the upcoming appearance in Scottsdale of a women's suffrage speaker, Scott said, "A good many of us men are coming to feel that we need the help of the women in Arizona as we enter the important work of founding a state and determining the principles that shall control us for years to come." For many Arizona leaders of the day such a statement was an anathema, but for Winfield Scott it made sense, and he did not hesitate to speak his mind.

When the regents' meeting concluded in Tucson, Scott went on to Socorro, New Mexico. He had decided to superintend the Socorro gold mining camp, and he left his ranch in the care of George Blount's

Douglas, Arizona Territory, at about the time Winfield Scott arrived to organize a Baptist congregation. (Arizona Department of Library, Archives and Public Records)

The University of Arizona as it looked in 1902 when Winfield Scott arrived to attend his first meeting as a member of the board of regents. (Arizona Historical Society)

brother Frank who had recently arrived from Illinois. His plans called
for returning to Scottsdale in December to help Helen move to the
mining camp, and in early December the Scotts said good-bye to their
Scottsdale friends. Scott vowed to return frequently. For the better
part of a year Scott commuted between Socorro, Tucson, and Scottsdale with frequent side trips to old Mexico. In February 1903 he returned to the valley by way of Magdalena, Sonora, where he inspected
the Coast Line Copper Company's group of claims adjoining La Gran
Proveedora, a property of the Arizona-Mexican Copper Company.
Scott had returned to escort the wife and daughter of his chief engineer
back to the Socorro camp, but while he was in the valley, he preached a
union service for the Christian and Baptist congregations in Phoenix.
Before leaving, he was the guest of honor at a dinner party given by his
friends the Elliotts. He would be sixty-five on February 26, and his
friends brought him a few presents, among them a monogrammed walk-
ing stick. As he grew older, Scott walked with an increasingly pronounced limp.

In early March, before beginning a trip east, Scott returned to the
Salt River Valley once more. On the way home he swung south into
Mexico on mining business and engaged in church work along the
border, most likely preaching in Douglas and Naco. Continuing toward
home he happened to be in Benson, Arizona, on a Sunday, and true to
form, he preached there also. After taking care of business in the
valley, Scott left Phoenix for Kansas to begin a four-month inspection
tour of some of the major universities of the Midwest and East. With a
view to gathering information that might prove useful in managing the
affairs of the University of Arizona, he made extended visits to four-
year schools in Kansas, Illinois, Indiana, Ohio, Pennsylvania, and
New York. In addition to his many inspection tours, Scott also attended the birthday celebration of the Baptist denomination held at
Buffalo and delivered the Memorial Day address in his home town of
Farmer Village. Before returning home, he visited his alma mater, the
University of Rochester, and attended commencement exercises. An
old friend, General Elwell S. Otis, presided as toastmaster that day and
surprised Scott by calling him from the audience to address the gradu-
ates. Scott reportedly made "the speech of the day," and it must have
pleased the former member of the Delphic Literary Society to be so
honored at his own school. The chaplain returned to Arizona in early
July, in time to attend a regents' meeting. The phrase "wandering up
and down the earth" does not adequately capture the pace of Scott's
travels; he seemed to be in perpetual motion.

On August 5, 1903, the Board of Regents of the University of
Arizona unanimously elected Winfield Scott chancellor of the univer-

sity. Apparent dissatisfaction over the university's administration had brought the resignations of the school's president and chancellor in late June and early July, and now the regents chose Scott to sit as their chairman for the remainder of his term on the board. As chancellor, Scott guided the deliberations of the regents until January 1905. Then, as now, it required skill and patience to guide the direction of the university, but Scott seems to have been equal to the task.

In late August Scott attended the national encampment of the G.A.R. in San Francisco and was elected chaplain-in-chief for the coming year. A man from such a small department as Arizona usually had little chance of being elected to a national post, but Scott received solid support from both the New York and Pacific Coast commanderies of the Military Order of the Loyal Legion of the United States, a branch of the G.A.R. composed of former Union officers. It was "a rare honor" dependent solely on his stature among his peers, but what pleased Scott most was the solid support he received from the Kansas delegation, especially since his opponent in the race came from Nebraska. His old comrades remembered his work in their states.

Helen Scott stayed in the Bay Area after the convention to visit her daughters and grandchildren, while her husband began another month-long journey. He traveled to Tucson to conduct a regents' meeting and continued on into old Mexico on mining business. It is clear from newspaper accounts of his travels that Scott no longer managed the Socorro gold mining property, but what became of his interests there is not known. His position as chancellor of the University of Arizona required his presence at all the meetings of the regents, and he now adjusted his schedule accordingly. Returning to the valley in the latter part of September, he made arrangements to live in Phoenix for the winter. Having lived away from home and friends for a year, it is possible Scott felt his wife now deserved what she yearned for, the social life of Phoenix.

The next year Winfield Scott divided his time between his monthly trip to Tucson to chair the regents' meeting and those activities that had been a part of his life for many years. He and his wife continued to live in Phoenix, in a cottage at Twenty-first Avenue and Madison, and ever alert to the opportunity to do Christian work, they helped organize a weekly prayer meeting in their neighborhood. Between commitments, Scott made quick trips to his ranch to check on his fields and orchards, and in the spring he received two letters that acknowledged different aspects of his varied and distinguished career. In April he received a letter from a party in Iowa addressed simply to Chaplain Winfield Scott and bearing no address or other designation. The letter came directly to the Phoenix Post Office without any rerouting, and regardless of its

Winfield Scott's Southwest, ca. 1905

importance to him, the letter has significance to the historian, because it indicates that all the speeches, letters, articles, and personal tours had thoroughly identified the promoter with his valley. In June he received notification that he had been promoted by order of President Roosevelt to "chaplain retired with the rank of major." All Civil War veterans with creditable records had been given promotions of one rank and pay grade, and Scott certainly qualified. Of the two letters, Scott undoubtedly prized the one from the War Department more highly, but one cannot help but marvel at the reputation of a man, in the age before mass media communication, whose name was also his address. August found the Scotts preparing for a long journey east, but after they first traveled to Tucson for a regents' meeting, Helen apparently did not feel up to making the rest of the trip. She remained in Tucson while her husband visited Kansas City, St. Louis, Chicago, Boston, and points in between.

Scott stopped in St. Louis to take in the World's Fair, and while there he visited a display detailing the irrigation systems of the Salt River Valley. It did not take long for a crowd to gather as he discoursed on points of interest in the display, and he spent an hour answering questions from curious onlookers. He was truly in his element acting as an informal host, and the sponsors of the display could not have hired a better guide.

In Boston, Scott attended the annual encampment of the Grand Army of the Republic and served the convention as chaplain-in-chief. To open the festivities, twenty-six thousand Union veterans marched through Boston while perhaps one million people lined the streets in the August sun. For the preacher who would have rather been a soldier, this pomp and ceremony undoubtedly marked a great moment in his life. Traveling on to Geneva, New York, Scott attended a reunion of the 126th New York Volunteers and addressed the one hundred ten members still able to make the trip. He also visited with his family, and although his mother and father had been gone for some years, there were still many sisters, nieces, nephews, and cousins to visit one last time. He would not be back again.

Scott returned to Arizona in mid-September to learn that he had been selected as a delegate to attend the Republican territorial convention in Prescott, and at the convention he once again received the Republican nomination to run for the legislature. Atypically for a politician, Scott had not run in 1900 or 1902, but he was back in harness now. As in 1898 he campaigned vigorously and received a strong endorsement from the *Arizona Republican,* but he did not win the election. The Prohibition party ran a full slate of candidates in Maricopa County and polled votes that normally might have gone to Scott. He may or may not have received all of those votes, but even three-fifths of them would have assured his election.

Chaplain Scott and his wife remained in Phoenix during the first six months of 1905. During the summer, while Helen Scott lived with her daughters in California, her husband traveled to Kansas and Oklahoma Territory on a sentimental visit. To describe a year in the life of Winfield Scott without mentioning an extended visit somewhere would seem unnatural. Among several stops in Kansas, Scott visited the town that bore his name, but which he had not seen in thirty-five years. In a glowing tribute to Scott's character and career, the *Winfield Courier* had this to say of the man, "His handshake is warm and hearty and his conversation bright and interesting. His whole personality sheds warmth and good will."

Scott spent most of his seven-week journey with his younger brother James, whom he had not seen in twenty years. James Sinclair Scott, or "Sink" to his family, lived in Beaver County, Oklahoma, and Winfield spent his time there preaching on Sunday and devoting the rest of the week to his brother. As happened in other generations of Scotts when brothers settled new lands, James and Winfield had not seen much of one another through the years and would not meet again. Distance, however, had separated them only by miles, and their few weeks together were good ones. Upon returning to the Salt River Valley, Winfield Scott headed home to Scottsdale. Except for summer trips to California, his days of wandering the earth were over.

CHAPTER XII

"*I leave to you my work in Scottsdale*"

Chaplain Winfield Scott may have ended his peripatetic travels, but his pace did not slow perceptibly. For the last five years of his life he stayed close to his ranch in Scottsdale, filling his days with church commitments, ranch work, and community involvement. He spent summers in California and occasionally traveled within Arizona, but his base remained in Scottsdale. If ever there was a place during his long career that he could call home, it was his ranch.

Over the next several years, Scott worked steadily to further develop his ranch. He began dairy farming again, gradually increasing his herd to approximately one hundred head, and made long-range plans with the acquisition of twenty calves. His alfalfa acreage easily fed the herd, and he had spare cuttings to sell for twelve dollars per ton. He also bought young feeder cattle, experimented with forage crops needed to fatten them, and had good success growing milo. Scott bought a hay baler and a McCormick binder to handle his hay and grain crops, and he built a large shed to store baled alfalfa. He also built a new barn as an addition to the hay shed, drilled a new well, and installed a large water tank and gasoline powered pump to provide water for the stock and for his home.

Scott worked like a young man just starting out, but as the years passed, it was farming and not preaching or promoting which betrayed his advancing years. In the fall of 1906 George Winfield Scott, George's son, came down from San Francisco with his wife and small son to help his uncle. Soon after their arrival Helen Scott held a community reception to introduce George's wife Ruby to the ladies of Scottsdale, and some time later the chaplain offered his nephew forty acres at well under the going price in an effort to persuade him to stay. The young Scotts, nevertheless, stayed just one winter and spring. Perhaps Ruby's health contributed to their decision to return to California, because she spent some time in a Phoenix hospital. Whatever the reason for their leaving, Scott found himself without a good man to run his operation, and the following September he leased his grainfields and pasture for five years to the Butts brothers. That move left him free to concentrate on his dairy operation and his fruit crops, but in the winter of 1909 he sold his entire dairy herd. He was not retiring, merely easing the load.

He continued tending his citrus trees, grapevines, and fruit trees; he exhibited his lemons at the territorial fair; and he presented the Phoenix Board of Trade with specimens of his Washington navel oranges before shipping them east. One day in the spring of 1908 a reporter for the *Arizona Gazette* went out to interview Scott about his long and varied career. He found the seventy-one-year-old parson repairing farm machinery, and while Scott worked, he regaled the reporter with stories of his life in the West. Between anecdotes, Scott talked enthusiastically about Scottsdale and its potential as a health resort and citrus farming community. He liked to talk about that more

George Winfield Scott, son of the chaplain's brother George Washington Scott, came to Scottsdale in 1906 to help his Uncle Winfield with his ranch. (Mrs. Ruby Scott Storz, Esparto, California)

than anything else. He never stopped promoting his town and his valley.

Upon his return home in late August 1905 he resurrected the idea of a "trolley line" to Phoenix and reiterated his belief that Scottsdale would become a "suburb of Phoenix." In early October, as health seekers and winter visitors began to arrive, the population of Scottsdale almost doubled. The resulting traffic between Scottsdale and Phoenix prompted two stage-line operators to initiate additional service to handle the increased load. In this prosperous atmosphere, Scott continued to push his plans for an interurban line to Phoenix, most likely soliciting subsidies from landowners along the route. The Panic of 1907 may have postponed his plans, but in late December it was reported that Scott was talking "trolley line" again and that the property owners in Scottsdale favored the plan. Finally, in 1909 his efforts began to generate concrete results. In February plans for a gasoline-powered streetcar line between Phoenix and Scottsdale were announced in the *Arizona Republican.* The line to Scottsdale represented the first phase in a system to link Phoenix, Scottsdale, Tempe, Mesa, and Glendale. The company, known as the Phoenix, Tempe and Mesa Motor Line, planned to run its tracks out McDowell Road and then along the Arizona Canal to Scottsdale. The line would pass the first winter resort in the Salt River Valley, Ingleside Inn, then under construction.* After the Phoenix-Scottsdale section became operative, the line would continue south to Tempe and Mesa, with a branch line to carry sugar beets from Scottsdale to Glendale for the Southwestern Sugar Beet Company. Half of the $125,000 needed to build the road was pledged before the plans were announced, and Scott bought five acres in the northwest corner of the Scottsdale townsite, probably in anticipation of success.

A new development occurred in March 1909 which the suburban railroad promoters may have anticipated. The Twenty-fifth Legislative Assembly passed a railroad tax exemption giving Arizona railroads constructed under the law a ten-year exemption from taxation. Winfield Scott immediately set about forming another new company, the Orange Belt and Scottsdale Railroad, which apparently superseded the Phoenix, Tempe and Mesa Motor Line. He subscribed to fifty-five shares of the new company's stock, amounting to $5,500 and enlisted ten other

---

*Ingleside Inn was built near the center of the Arizona Improvement Company's original orange orchard, less than a mile east of the modern intersection of 56th Street and Indian School Road. Property owned by the Improvement Company adjacent to the grove allowed for the immediate construction of tennis courts and riding stables and the eventual construction of an eighteen-hole golf course and a polo field. Apparently resurrecting the original "Orangedale" concept, a townsite was also platted, adjacent to the inn on the south. These various developments, proposed and completed, filled eight hundred acres bounded by 56th Street on the west, the new crosscut canal on the east, Indian School Road on the north, and Thomas Road on the south.

men from Phoenix and Scottsdale to subscribe to an additional fifty-eight shares. This pledge of $11,300 amounted to little more than $1,000 per mile for the ten-mile line* and did not begin to approach the $15,000 per mile needed to build and outfit the line. Scott apparently had some success, however, with property owners who had subscribed in the first company, because an April 11 newspaper article, in referring to the company's $150,000 capitalization, stated that "a good part . . . [of it] has been taken up in the city [Phoenix] and by property owners along the route." Prior to this good news, the original subscribers met on March 30, 1909, and elected Winfield Scott, Charles Miller, N. A. Morford, L. J. Rice, and Frank T. Alkire as their board of directors. The board, in turn, elected Scott, president; Rice, vice-president; Morford, secretary; and Alkire, treasurer.

Scott's success in raising money appears to have been more than mere publicity, because his activities forced Moses H. Sherman, owner of the Phoenix street railway system, to admit he had made a mistake in not encouraging Scott to join him. From Los Angeles Sherman wrote to his Phoenix manager concerning Scott's progress, "We would have gotten all the money that he has raised for an extension to the Falls and we ought to have done it, in place of letting him build an 'opposition' road." The falls of which Sherman writes were on the Arizona Canal about two miles west of Scottsdale near the Ingleside Inn. Sherman went on to write that he felt confident he could eventually take over the new road, but he did not get the opportunity. With Scott's death a year later, the idea died also.

Concurrent with his long push to get Scottsdale a rail connection with Phoenix, Scott engaged in a multitude of other activities. In 1906 he presided over the convention of the Arizona Baptist Association, was elected vice-commander of the Arizona G.A.R., and received an interim appointment as general missionary and secretary to the missionary board of the territorial Baptist convention, a position he had not held since his Kansas days. He served on the first board of the Arizona Canal Water Users' Association, and in the fall of 1906 he ran once again for the territorial legislature. Scott campaigned vigorously against a proposal for joint Arizona-New Mexico statehood and received the warm endorsement of not only the *Arizona Republican*, but the Democratic *Arizona Gazette* as well. The *Republican* praised his service to the territory's school system, remarked that in the twentieth legislature he was "admittedly one of the best, if not the best, parliamentarian" and closed with these thoughts:

---

*The proposed line began at the intersection of Seventh Street and Van Buren and traveled a north, northeasterly course to approximately the intersection of Sixteenth Street and Indian School Road. There it turned east and ran seven miles along Indian School Road to the Scottsdale townsite.

The falls of the Arizona Canal. When the Phoenix newspapers first began to mention Winfield Scott's ranch in their columns, they often described it as being about a mile and a half east of the falls. Today, the remnants of the falls can be seen just a short distance northeast of the modern intersection of **56th Street and Indian School Road.** (Historical Collection of Herb and Dorothy McLaughlin, Phoenix, Arizona)

Ingleside Inn, when completed in 1909, was the first resort in the Salt River Valley. The main club house, pictured here, was 150 feet long, finished in grey stucco, and contained dining rooms, living rooms, offices, a kitchen, and a limited number of guest rooms on the second floor. Guest cottages provided the main accommodations, and a corner of one of them is visible on the far right. The Orange Belt and Scottsdale Railroad was to have run by the inn, making it one of the major stops on the line. The entrance to the tree-covered driveway of Ingleside Inn was six-tenths of a mile east of the falls of the Arizona Canal, along what whould become Indian School Road. (Arizona Department of Library, Archives and Public Records)

> Chaplain Scott is the same large hearted, fair minded campaigner that he is citizen and neighbor. He is sound and out spoken [*sic*] on all the vital issues of this campaign. . . . If elected he will be better qualified to serve the people than ever before and can be counted on to do wisely.

Scott was on the right side of the joint statehood issue but in the wrong party. Joint statehood was defeated, but the Democrats captured all but a handful of legislative seats in the territory, and, except for the office of probate judge, they swept the ticket in Maricopa County.

Scott devoted the following year primarily to farming, but he also served as department chaplain for the G.A.R. and continued his work as general missionary for the Baptist convention. He worked on his "trolley" plans, gave the Fourth of July address in Tempe, attended a Baptist celebration in Tucson, and preached in the Scottsdale schoolhouse. As the Baptist churches in the valley began to realize that Chaplain Scott would remain at home on something approaching a permanent basis, the invitations to preach began to pour in.

Between farming and preaching he made the time to give a series of lectures on the Civil War to the Scottsdale schoolchildren. These stories were geared primarily to the eighth graders in the one-room schoolhouse, but Scott let the little ones come up and feel the indentation in his right shin where the musket ball had lodged during the battle at Maryland Heights. He also found time to travel to Nogales for a meeting of the directors of the Coast Line Copper Company. Apparently this mining venture had enjoyed more success than previous Scott speculations.* The old chaplain devoted the greater part of the winter and spring of 1908, however, to preaching. Once again, he assisted the Tempe Baptists when their pastor fell ill in February. During March Scott commuted to West End, a little settlement southwest of Phoenix, where he preached every Sunday and assisted the Reverend R. D. Latter, the Arizona Baptist colporteur, in a series of meetings designed to bring in new members. During April and May he preached in Mesa, Tempe, Scottsdale, Glendale, and Fowler, a little farm community near Glendale. Of Scott's commitments around the valley, Verner Vanderhoof wrote simply, "Chaplain is very much in demand this spring and is apt to be most any place at any time."

During his last five summers, Scott could always be found in California. The marriage of Florence Margaret Scott to LeGrande Turner in June 1906 turned into a summer-long family reunion in the San Francisco area. Minnie Scott Albright journeyed from Fort Bliss, Texas, where her husband was stationed and met her parents en route on the Southern Pacific. The marriage took place in Los Gatos, near

---

*When Scott's will was later probated, his ninety-nine thousand Coast Line shares were valued at ten cents each.

A Washington's Birthday gathering in Winfield Scott's grove, 1906. In the first row Elsie Elliott stands to the viewer's right of the flag in a white dress. In the second row Mrs. Mittie Hayden, wife of Scottsdale's Wilford Hayden, is the fourth woman from the viewer's left, Mrs. Minnie Elliott the fifth, and Helen Scott the seventh. The Reverend Judson A. Elliott can be seen just over Mrs. Elliott's left shoulder wearing a bow tie, and Chaplain Scott is the third man from the viewer's right in the second row. (Mrs. Ruth M. Elliott, Phoenix, Arizona)

San Jose, at the home of Helen Scott Flint, who had moved from Oakland with her family. In the several years since moving to Hayward, Florence Scott had become chairman of the high school science department, coached the girls' basketball team to an undefeated season, and made a name for herself as an active worker in Christian causes. She had also won the heart of a prominent gentleman from Hayward. Considering the time and travel required to see one another, it is not surprising that the reunion turned into an all-summer affair.

In June of 1908, with Minnie Scott Albright and her husband once again returned from the Philippines and stationed in San Diego, the Scotts decided to summer there instead of northern California. Finding the area much to their liking, they soon bought a lot in the new suburb of Normal Heights and built a two-story home amid tents, unpaved streets, and vacant lots. Scott's summer "vacation" proved to be much like his "retirement," and while spending the summer in San Diego, he engaged in mission work under the Reverend Dr. H. B. Hinson and took on the responsibility of a small Sunday school in the Adams Avenue schoolhouse in Normal Heights.

The following summer Scott began preaching services in the schoolhouse, and as the congregation grew, he bought two lots on the corner of Madison Avenue·and Hawley Boulevard and made plans to erect a chapel. In October 1910, before he returned to Scottsdale, he signed a contract for the construction of the chapel, which would cost several thousand dollars. Scott planned to pay for it out of his salary earned while preaching there, but only three weeks later, he suddenly became ill and died. Unlike the Orange Belt and Scottsdale Railroad, however, the idea for the chapel did not die with him. Helen Scott took up the cause of the new church and assumed a $1,000 mortgage on her new home to see it built. Scott Memorial Chapel was completed in February 1911, and with the help of friends and family, Helen Scott solicited contributions to pay off the mortgage. She presented a clear title to the congregation in June 1913, and for the last twenty years of her life, Helen Scott devoted her energies to the church her husband started in the Adams Avenue schoolhouse. The little chapel has become Scott Memorial Baptist Church, with the largest congregation in San Diego County. As part of its ministry, Scott Memorial supports and operates a Christian elementary school, a four-year Christian high school, and a four-year Christian liberal arts college.* Nothing could have pleased the Scotts more.

---

*Approximately 2,500 people attend Scott Memorial's six Sunday morning services which are held at two locations in San Diego and El Cajon. In addition, 400 students attend Scott Memorial's Christian Heritage College, 850 are enrolled at its Christian High School, and more than 200 youngsters attend its elementary school which is housed in various churches in the San Diego area.

Scott Memorial Chapel, built in the Normal Heights section of San Diego, 1910–1911, by Chaplain and Mrs. Winfield Scott. (Scott Memorial Baptist Church)

In January 1909 Winfield Scott called a meeting of the Scottsdale community to be held at his home. He hoped to organize a group that would bring the growing community together for social fellowship and entertainment, and the thirty-four assembled residents unanimously supported the idea. The Scottsdale Social Union came into being with Winfield Scott elected chairman. The idea behind the union stemmed from the same roots as the idea behind the union services on Sunday. Winfield Scott wanted his small community to live and work together in harmony with no denominational division. Elsie Elliott Severance remembers her mother, Minnie, urging Scott to form a Baptist church in Scottsdale. She thought it would be fitting for everyone, regardless of their own denomination, to join the Baptist church, but Scott knew that such a proposal would be divisive and let Minnie's repeated urgings go unheeded. The social union represented a positive link to bind the community together, to help it pull together for the future.

In April, just a week before the announcement of the Orange Belt and Scottsdale Railroad, Scott went before the Scottsdale School Board. Although the school population of the district had increased by only eleven students since 1896, Scott believed in the future of Scottsdale and in the role education would play in that future. He urged that a substantial brick schoolhouse be built as an indication of Scottsdale's commitment to the future, and the board agreed. They called a bond election, and a $5,000 bond issue passed with fourteen votes in favor and none opposed.[1] In September sealed construction bids were opened, and while Scott worked long hours to insure the success of the railroad line to Phoenix, construction began on the Scottsdale Grammar School. In late January 1910, with the red brick schoolhouse* complete, the community made plans to celebrate its dedication. An early February date chosen conflicted with an aviation show in Phoenix and had to be changed, but that allowed a more appropriate date to be used. On February 26, 1910, Winfield Scott's seventy-third birthday, the new schoolhouse received its christening. Following a sumptuously served picnic in the school's basement, several hundred people gathered for the program upstairs, with many having to stand outside to listen. Arizona Governor Richard E. Sloan and Indiana Governor Thomas R. Marshall were present to address the crowd, as were school officials from Phoenix and Tempe, including Professor Arthur J. Matthews, president of the Normal School of Arizona. Chaplain Scott presided over the dedication and "discoursed happily on the pride and progress of the district." He must have been an extremely proud man that day. His oasis in the desert had become a prospering community with a bright future.

In March a new board of directors for the Orange Belt and Scottsdale Railroad Company took office. Albert G. Utley, the Scottsdale townsite owner and one of the original subscribers to the railroad stock, took a seat on the board, and Scott was again elected president.

Seemingly never the one to lose his enthusiasm for horticultural experiments, Scott planted one hundred Valencia orange trees with the idea that if they did well, he would plant several acres in Valencias the next spring. After attending the territorial Baptist convention in mid-April, Scott left for San Diego with his wife in early May.

In September, during the campaign to elect delegates to the Arizona constitutional convention, Scott wrote a letter from San Diego to the *Arizona Gazette*. Harry R. Tritle, editor of the *Gazette*, published the letter on the front page under the headline **WINFIELD SCOTT RAISES VOICE FOR PEOPLE.** In anticipation of statehood, the people of Arizona were being asked to decide which party should govern the constitutional convention and thereby control the writing of the constitution. The leaders of the Republican party in Arizona tested the political waters in Washington and decreed that in order for Arizona to gain statehood, the constitution must be conservative. The initiative, referendum, and recall could not be included, and the Republican party pledged to see that they were not. The Democratic leadership in Arizona, conversely, tested the political waters in Arizona and found that the people wanted the initiative, referendum, and recall.

*The red brick schoolhouse still stands today on the Scottsdale Mall, housing the Scottsdale Chamber of Commerce.

Almost the entire student body in front of the red brick Scottsdale Grammar School, ca. 1912. In 1976, the "Little Red Schoolhouse" became the first building on the Arizona Register of Historic Places. Identifying those in the picture: First Row (l. to r.) leg of an unknown, mischievous boy on horseback, Alvin Brown and Helen Hayden on horseback, Edward "Buster" Graves, Mary Graves, Nina Bassham, Frank Coldwell, George "Bud" Service, James Vanderhoof, Lenore Coldwell, Adeline Coldwell, Carl Bassham, Nora Holmes, John Elmer Williams, Polly Elliott, William "Willy" Miller, Tom Coldwell, Laura Elliott. Second Row (l. to r.) Mrs. Frank Last, teacher, behind "Bud" Service, George Thomas in hat, unknown boy, Ellsworth "Brownie" Brown, Myrtle Elliott, Stanley Ellis Thomas, May Vanderhoof holding her horse. Third Row (l. to r.) Grace Thomas behind her brother George, Ruth Brown behind her brother "Brownie," and Mrs. Walter P. Smith in hat. (Frank Coldwell, Silver City, New Mexico)

In an attempt to make political capital out of the Republican stand against these progressive measures, Harry Tritle wrote an article for his newspaper recalling that the Republicans had supported the initiative and referendum in their 1898 convention and mentioning that Winfield Scott had enthusiastically endorsed those reform tools during the ensuing campaign. Apparently stung by the inference that he had deserted his principles, Scott wrote Tritle and strongly affirmed his progressive ideals. He had been a Republican all of his adult life and had faithfully served the party in Arizona for fourteen years, but on the issue of a progressive or a conservative constitution, he now parted company with the Republican leadership and said so in the *Gazette*.

> I do not advise men to leave their parties, but if their parties will not do at this time, what the better judgement of the people believe ought to be done, just fall back on the right of every American citizen and practice in this election "The divine right of scratching."

The term *scratching* originated in early nineteenth century American politics and meant that if the party's candidate was not acceptable, scratch out the name and write in one that was acceptable. Scott's advice to his fellow Republicans was simple: renounce the party leadership. Harry Tritle wrote Scott that his letter "did more than any article written or speech made to influence the voters to vote right." Whatever the case may be, all nine Republicans, including such respected figures as Joseph H. Kibbey and Dwight B. Heard, were defeated in Maricopa County.

The day after the election, in a letter to his brother George, Scott spoke more directly.

> The Republicans had the best chance in the world to play a winning card, but the bosses were unwilling to trust the people, and tried to rule them, and the people took the bit in their teeth and ran away with the whole business. The day is past for bosses and corporations determined to rule and cinch the people.

Having made arrangements for the construction of his chapel in San Diego, Winfield Scott returned to Scottsdale on October 4, 1910. Helen Scott was expected home soon, and to his friends, Scott looked well. Two weeks later, on October 17, he suddenly became quite ill. Rushed to St. Joseph's Hospital in Phoenix with what was at first thought to be food poisoning, Scott's condition deteriorated rapidly and surgery became necessary. A strangulated hernia, the result of scar tissue from an old Civil War wound, was found blocking the intestinal tract and was successfully removed. The shock and exhaustion occasioned by the ordeal proved to be too much even for the tough old chaplain, and in spite of his doctors' optimism, Scott knew he was dying. Although he had made a will in 1904, he now wrote a special testament to the people of Scottsdale.

> My Dear Neighbors and Friends:
>   As I feel myself drawing near to the other world, my heart goes out to you every one, young and old, with a longing I have never known before. I have a few things which have made my life rich, and I have now but one desire; that is that you all may enjoy them with me.

He bequeathed several Christian ideas to his friends and then ended with one last bequest.

> I leave to you my work in Scottsdale. I had planned to do much this winter with you, but God has called me. If you take this work and do it, and enlarge it as God gives you strength, you will receive my blessing and His.

At 9:00 P.M. on October 19, 1910, Chaplain Winfield Scott slipped quietly away.

Just the previous Memorial Day, Scott, who always considered himself an old soldier, made arrangements to be buried in the G.A.R. section of the Mount Hope Cemetery in San Diego. It was there that Helen Scott would take him in the spring of 1911, when she said good-bye to Arizona for the last time. Immediately following his death, however, the Reverend C. J. Banks, the preacher from Ohio who had lived on Scott's ranch while regaining his health, conducted the funeral service in the First Baptist Church in Phoenix. After the service, an honor guard from the Phoenix G.A.R. post escorted the casket to the holding vault at the Rosedale Cemetery, and during the G.A.R. service there, the bugler sounded reveille instead of the traditional taps. Scott wanted everyone to think of him not as at rest but as entering a new life.

The day before the funeral the people of Scottsdale held their own memorial service as an expression of community sadness, love, and respect. At that service and others, there were many eulogies and glowing tributes to Scott, but the schoolchildren of Scottsdale said what mattered most. In school they were asked to write on the topic, "Why we loved Chaplain Scott." In reply, some of them wrote,

> Because Chaplain loved us.
> Because Chaplain was good to us.
> Because Chaplain gave us so many things.
> Chaplain took time to come over and tell us war stories
>   when he was very busy.
> Chaplain fought for our country.
> Chaplain improved our school grounds.
> Chaplain loved our flag.
> Chaplain helped us with our school plays.
> Chaplain gave us a party.
> Chaplain was our Santa Claus.

Chaplain Winfield Scott spent half a century in service to his God, his country, and his fellowman. He traveled across half a continent building churches, organizing congregations, and promoting the kingdom of God on earth. He had been a soldier, an army chaplain, an innovative farmer, an unlucky speculator, a dedicated educator, a progressive politician, and an enthusiastic and loving promoter of his town. And in the end his young friends said it all.

Notes to Chapters

NOTES TO CHAPTER I

1. Silvio A. Bedini, *Ridgefield in Review* (Ridgefield, Conn.: Ridgefield 250th Anniversary Committee, 1958), p. 48; Daniel W. Teller, *The History of Ridgefield Connecticut* (Danbury, Conn.: T. Donovan, 1878), p. 21.

2. James M. Guinn, *History of the State of California and Biographical Record of the Sacramento Valley, California* (Chicago: Chapman Publishing Co., 1906), p. 351.

3. Thomas J. Gregory, *History of Yolo County, California* (Los Angeles: Historic Record Co., 1913), p. 430.

4. DeForeest B. Wright, "The Story of Winfield Scott," typescript (Hollywood, Calif.: DeForeest B. Wright, 1970), p. 3.

5. David C. Smith, "Middle Range Farming in the Civil War Era: Life on a Farm in Seneca County, 1862–1866," *New York History* 48 (October, 1967):353–54, 359.

6. Lewis Halsey, *History of the Seneca Baptist Association* (Ithaca: Journal Association Book and Job Printing House, 1879), p. 133.

7. Arthur J. May, "History of the University of Rochester," typescript (Rochester: Department of Rare Books, Manuscripts and Archives, Rush Rhees Library, University of Rochester, 1964–68), chap. 4, pp. 2–4.

8. Halsey, *Seneca Baptist Association*, p. 69.

NOTES TO CHAPTER II

1. Bruce Catton, *Terrible Swift Sword* (Garden City, N. Y.: Doubleday and Co., 1963), pp. 403–05.

2. Lewis Halsey, *History of the Seneca Baptist Association* (Ithaca: Journal Association Book and Job Printing House, 1879), pp. 266–67; Arabella M. Willson, *Disaster, Struggle, Triumph* (Albany: Argus Co., 1870), pp. 435–55.

3. *Dictionary of American Biography*, rev. ed., s.v. "Lounsbury, Thomas Raynesford."

4. Willson, *Disaster, Struggle, Triumph*, p. 375.

5. Frederick Phisterer, comp., *New York in the War of the Rebellion, 1861 to 1865*, 3d ed., 5 vols. (Albany: J. B. Lyon Co., 1912), 4:3509.

6. Catton, *Terrible Swift Sword*, pp. 446–47. Citation also includes the information in the following paragraph.

7. Thomas R. Lounsbury, "In the Defenses of Washington," *Yale Review*, n. s. 2 (April, 1913):387–89, 403–10. Citation also includes the general background material in the following paragraphs dealing with the time spent by the 126th New York in the defenses of Washington.

8. Bruce Catton, *Never Call Retreat* (Garden City, N. Y.: Doubleday and Co., 1965), pp. 163–64.

9. Lounsbury, "In the Defenses of Washington," p. 411.

10. Catton, *Never Call Retreat*, pp. 178–79.

11. New York Monuments Commission for the Battlefields of Gettysburg and Chattanooga, *Final Report on the Battlefield of Gettysburg*, 3 vols. (Albany: J. B. Lyon Co., 1902), 2:905–06; Bruce Catton, *The Glory Road* (Garden City, N. Y.: Doubleday and Co., 1952), p. 296.

12. Catton, *The Glory Road*, p. 310.

13. Catton, *Never Call Retreat*, pp. 187–89.

14. Catton, *The Glory Road*, p. 312.

15. New York Monuments Commission, *Final Report,* p. 908.

16. Catton, *The Glory Road,* pp. 322–23.

17. Bruce Catton, *This Hallowed Ground* (Garden City, N. Y.: Doubleday and Co., 1956), pp. 320–22. Citation also includes general information on the Wilderness in the following paragraph.

18. Catton, *Never Call Retreat,* p. 358.

19. Catton, *This Hallowed Ground,* p. 329.

20. Catton, *Never Call Retreat,* pp. 358–59.

21. Bruce Catton, *A Stillness at Appomattox* (Garden City, N. Y.: Doubleday and Co., 1953), pp. 117, 121–27.

22. James Sullivan, *History of New York State,* 5 vols. (New York: Lewis Historical Publishing Co., 1927), 4:1736.

NOTES TO CHAPTER III

1. Earl F. Stover, *Up from Handymen–The U.S. Army Chaplaincy, 1865–1920* (Washington, D.C.: Office of the Chief of Chaplains, Department of the Army, 1977), chap. 3, p. 1.

2. David G. Taylor, "Boom Town Leavenworth: The Failure of the Dream," *The Kansas Historical Quarterly* 38 (Winter, 1972):392–93, 411–12, 414; Henry Pickering Walker, *The Wagonmasters* (Norman: University of Oklahoma Press, 1966), pp. 55, 58–59.

3. Taylor, "Boom Town Leavenworth," pp. 411–12.

4. Margaret Whittemore, *Historic Kansas* (Lawrence: University of Kansas Press, 1954), p. 128; Federal Writers' Project, *Kansas,* (New York: Viking Press, 1939), p. 238.

5. Alfred T. Andreas, *History of the State of Kansas* (Chicago: A. T. Andreas, 1883), p. 1589.

NOTES TO CHAPTER IV

1. W. B. Vickers, *History of the City of Denver, Arapahoe County, and Colorado* (Chicago: O. L. Baskin and Co., 1880), pp. 221–22, 27, 78; Maud Stevens, *A Century of Baptist Faith, 1864–1964* (Denver: First Baptist Church of Denver, 1963), p. 3; Bruce Keith Blunt, "Ninety Years of Baptist Missionary Administration in Colorado" (Th.D. diss., Central Baptist Theological Seminary, 1951), p. 14.

2. Vickers, *History of Denver,* p. 224.

3. Clarence W. Kemper, *The Story of "Old First"* (Denver, 1938), p. 13. Citation also includes the next two direct quotations.

4. Vickers, *History of Denver,* p. 278.

5. Federal Writers' Project, *Colorado,* (New York: Hastings House, 1941), pp. 276–77; Jerome C. Smiley, ed., *History of Denver* (1901; reprint ed., Denver: Colorado State Historical Society, 1971), p. 275.

6. Muriel Sibell Wolle, *Stampede to Timberline* (Boulder, Colo.: Muriel S. Wolle, 1949), pp. 17, 106; Smiley, *History of Denver,* p. 597.

7. Charles Howard Hopkins, *The Rise of the Social Gospel in American Protestantism 1865–1915* (New Haven: Yale University Press, 1940), pp. 3, 19.

8. Kemper, *The Story of "Old First",* pp. 13–14. Citation includes both direct quotations in the paragraph.

9. Stevens, *A Century of Baptist Faith,* p. 20.

NOTES TO CHAPTER V

1. James M. Guinn, *A History of California and an Extended History of Los Angeles and Environs*, 3 vols. (Los Angeles: Historic Record Co., 1915), 1:277; Andrew F. Rolle, *California*, 2d ed. (New York: Thomas Y. Crowell Co., 1969), p. 285.

2. M. M. Marberry, *The Golden Voice* (New York: Farrar, Straus and Co., 1947), p. 227.

3. Sanford Fleming, *For the Making of Ministers* (Valley Forge, Pa.: Judson Press, 1963), pp. 20–21.

4. Marberry, *The Golden Voice*, pp. 44, 48, 140–61, 193, 198–99, 214–16.

5. David F. Myrick, *Railroads of Arizona*, vol. 1 (Berkeley: Howell-North Books, 1975), p. 16.

6. Guinn, *History of California* 1:277; Rolle, *California*, p. 359.

7. Tom Hughes, *History of Banning and San Gorgonio Pass* (Banning, Calif.: Banning Record Printers, ca. 1938), pp. 17–18, 22. Citation also includes the general information on Banning in the following paragraphs.

8. Erwin G. Gudde, *California Place Names*, 2d ed. (Berkeley and Los Angeles: University of California Press, 1960), p. 21.

9. Hughes, *History of Banning*, pp. 22–23.

10. Rolle, *California*, pp. 359–60; Warren A. Beck and David A. Williams, *California* (Garden City, N. Y.: Doubleday and Co., 1972), p. 287; John W. Caughey, *California*, 3d ed. (Englewood Cliffs, N. J.: Prentice-Hall, 1970), p. 354.

11. Marberry, *The Golden Voice*, pp. 229–30.

12. Caughey, *California*, pp. 329–30.

13. Marberry, *The Golden Voice*, pp. 234–42. Citation also includes general Kalloch material in the rest of the paragraph.

14. Caughey, *California*, pp. 328–29.

15. William Cathcart, ed., *The Baptist Encyclopedia* (Philadelphia: Louis H. Everts, 1881), p. 1036.

16. Marberry, *The Golden Voice*, pp. 235–320, 322–30, 338–41. Citation includes material in this paragraph and the first sentence in the next.

NOTES TO CHAPTER VI

1. Myron Angel, ed., *History of Nevada* (Oakland: Thompson and West, 1881), p. 218, 633–34, 640. Citation also includes material on Reno in the third paragraph of this chapter.

2. Samuel P. Davis, ed., *The History of Nevada*, 2 vols. (Los Angeles: Elms Publishing Co., 1913), 1:538.

3. George F. Warren and Frank A. Pearson, *Prices* (New York: John Wiley and Sons, 1933), p. 197.

NOTES TO CHAPTER VII

1. Robert W. Frazer, *Forts of the West* (Norman: University of Oklahoma Press, 1965), p. 171.

2. Federal Writers' Project, *Washington* (Portland, Oreg.: Binfords and Mort, 1941), p. 217.

3. Martha Summerhayes, *Vanished Arizona*, 4th ed. (Tucson: Arizona Silhouettes, 1960), p. 182.

NOTES TO CHAPTER VIII

1. Hubert Howe Bancroft, *History of Arizona and New Mexico, 1530–1888* (San Francisco: History Co., 1889), p. 623.

2. Jay J. Wagoner, *Arizona Territory, 1863–1912* (Tucson: University of Arizona Press, 1970), pp. 215–16.

3. Robert W. Frazer, *Forts of the West* (Norman: University of Oklahoma Press, 1965), p. 26.

4. Patrick C. Henderson, "The Public Domain in Arizona: 1863–1891" (Ph.D. diss., University of New Mexico, 1965), pp. 78, 81; Benjamin Horace Hibbard, *A History of the Public Land Policies* (1924; reprint ed., New York: Peter Smith, 1939), p. 429.

5. Dan L. Thrapp, *The Conquest of Apacheria* (Norman: University of Oklahoma Press, 1967), pp. 312, 321, 359–60; Edward H. Peplow, Jr., *History of Arizona*, 3 vols. (New York: Lewis Historical Publishing Co., 1958), 1:412; Frazer, *Forts of the West*, p. 9.

NOTES TO CHAPTER IX

1. *Portrait and Biographical Record of Arizona* (Chicago: Chapman Publishing Co., 1901), p. 37.

2. James M. Barney, "The Early Annals of Scottsdale," *The Sheriff Magazine* 13 (June, 1954):53.

3. Wilburn W. Dick, "The History of the Scottsdale School System at Scottsdale, Arizona, 1896–1944" (M. A. thesis, Arizona State Teachers College, 1944), pp. 24–25.

4. Stephen C. Shadegg, *Century One* (Phoenix: W. A. Krueger, 1969), pp. 14–15.

NOTES TO CHAPTER X

1. Samuel Eliot Morison and Henry Steele Commager, *The Growth of the American Republic*, 5th ed., rev. and enl., 2 vols. (New York: Oxford University Press, 1962), 2:465.

NOTES TO CHAPTER XI

1. Robert S. Jeffrey, "The History of Douglas, Arizona" (M. A. thesis, University of Arizona, 1951), pp. 6–7, 11, 14–15.

2. Robert Glass Cleland, *A History of Phelps Dodge 1834–1950* (New York: Alfred A. Knopf, 1952), p. 109; Jo Connors, comp., *Who's Who in Arizona* (Tucson: Jo Connors, 1913), p. 113.

3. C. L. Sonnichsen, *Colonel Greene and the Copper Skyrocket* (Tucson: University of Arizona Press, 1974), pp. 59, 71–75, 114.

NOTES TO CHAPTER XII

1. Wilburn W. Dick, "The History of the Scottsdale School System at Scottsdale, Arizona, 1896–1944" (M. A. thesis, Arizona State Teachers College, 1944), pp. 37–38.

Bibliography

Bibliographic Essay

The following bibliography contains all of the sources, both primary and secondary, utilized in the preparation of this book. The absence of the personal papers of Winfield Scott presents the one obvious gap in the material. In 1895 all of Scott's letters, sermons, and personal records burned in a fire on his Scottsdale ranch, and the papers from his last fifteen years have failed to surface in the course of research for this book. The only substantive source of Scott writings is contained in the National Archives in Washington, D.C., where can be found his monthly chaplain's reports to the adjutant general of the United States and the many letters he wrote in his effort to gain a chaplain's post. Copies of these letters and reports are now on file in the Scottsdale Public Library.

The newspapers of Scott's time are the only other major source of Scott thought and deed. Wherever he went, the daily papers chronicled his life in detail and quoted extensively from his sermons, political speeches, and interviews. My research assistants and I have carefully read the newspapers listed in this bibliography, and unless specified as selected issues, the years listed for each newspaper have been read in their entirety.

The reader will note that only the main titles of books have been included in this bibliography. This has been done strictly in the interests of economy, for many books written during the late nineteenth and early twentieth centuries contained subtitles that stretched on interminably. Those wishing to know the full titles should consult my master's thesis on file in the Charles Trumbull Hayden Library at Arizona State University, Tempe, Arizona.

In addition, there are several sources utilized in the preparation of this book which do not conform to standard bibliographic entries. This material was researched by someone other than the author or his assistant, with the resulting notes forwarded to the project. Rather than create a special category in the body of the bibliography, I have included these special cases here. Karl Kabelac, assistant librarian for rare books, manuscripts and archives at the University of Rochester Library, researched the minutes of the meetings of the Delphic Literary Society for the four years Winfield Scott was a member. Henrene George, records management supervisor for the American Baptist Churches at Valley Forge, Pennsylvania, studied the minute books of the board of the American Baptist Home Missionary Society from late 1864 through late 1881 and recorded all references to Winfield Scott contained in the discussions and votes of the board. Evelyn Kirmse, assistant to the president of the University of Arizona, read the minutes of the board of regents of the university for Scott's 1902–1905 term on the board and forwarded her notes and comments to me. These three sets of information are on file in the Scottsdale Public Library.

A second category of material presented here rather than in the body of the bibliography comes from a group of interested individuals and Scott family relatives. They have generously shared genealogical information, newspaper clippings, letters, and notes relating to Winfield Scott and the Scott family. From Yvonne Green of Daly City, California; William Chapman of Winters, California; and Bula Mae Saunders of Ukiah, California, came genealogical charts, newspaper articles, copies of pages from family Bibles and collected notes. From Maurice L. Patterson of Interlaken, New York, came additional genealogical and historical information, and from Carl W. Fischer of Bayside, New York, genealogical material. From Lena Scott Polglase of Santa Cruz, California, came a small but vital group of Scott family letters. Finally, from DeForeest B. Wright of Hollywood, California, came informative newspaper clippings and additional genealogical material. Again, this information is on file in the Scottsdale Public Library.

In conclusion, I have attached a list of the repositories from which information and photographs have been collected. Anyone wishing to pursue his own study of Winfield Scott can consult these libraries and depositories for further information.

MAJOR DEPOSITORIES AND LIBRARIES

American Baptist Churches U.S.A., Valley Forge, Pennsylvania.

American Baptist Historical Society, Rochester, New York.

Arizona Historical Foundation, Arizona State University, Tempe.

Arizona Historical Society, Tucson.

Arizona Department of Library, Archives and Public Records, Phoenix.

Bancroft Library, University of California, Berkeley.

California Historical Society, San Francisco.

Charles Trumbull Hayden Library, Arizona State University, Tempe.

Denver Public Library, Western History Department.

Detroit Public Library, Burton Historical Collection.

Geneva Historical Society and Museum, Geneva, New York.

Interlaken Historical Society, Interlaken, New York.

Kansas State Historical Society, Topeka.

Los Angeles County Museum of Natural History.

Middlebury Historical Society, Wyoming, New York.

National Archives, Washington, D.C.

Nevada State Historical Society, Reno.

New York Historical Society, New York, New York.

Onandaga Historical Association, Syracuse, New York.

Oregon Historical Society, Portland.

Sanford Fleming Library, American Baptist Seminary of the West, Berkeley, California.

Scottsdale Historical Society.

Scottsdale Public Library.

Sharlot Hall Historical Society, Prescott, Arizona.

Sherman Foundation Research Library, Corona del Mar, California.

University of Rochester Library, Rochester, New York.

PRIMARY SOURCES

Manuscript Collections

Corona del Mar, California. Sherman Foundation Research Library. M. H. Sherman Papers.

Detroit, Michigan. Detroit Public Library, Burton Historical Collection. Winfield Scott Papers, 1819–1886, in the Jackson Family Papers. Xerographic copy on file in the Scottsdale Public Library.

Rochester, New York. University of Rochester Library, Department of Rare Books, Manuscripts and Archives. Selected University Records. Xerographic copies on file in the Scottsdale Public Library.

Sacramento, California. California State Library. Records of the Families of California Pioneers. Vol. 6. Winfield Scott.

Tempe, Arizona. Arizona State University Archives. Minutes [of the Board of Education of the Normal School of Arizona at Tempe].

Government Documents

Federal

Biographical Directory of the American Congress, 1774–1971. Washington, D.C.: Government Printing Office, 1971.

Heitman, Francis B. *Historical Register and Dictionary of the United States Army, From its Organization, September 29, 1879, to March 2, 1903.* 2 vols. Washington, D.C.: Government Printing Office, 1903.

United States, Census Office:
Population Schedules of the 6th Census of the United States, 1840. Michigan, Oakland County, Town of Novi.

Population Schedules of the 7th Census of the United States, 1850. New York, Seneca County, Town of Ovid.

Population Schedules of the 8th Census of the United States, 1860. New York, Seneca County, Town of Ovid, Post Office of Farmer.

Population Schedules of the 9th Census of the United States, 1870. New York, Seneca County, Town of Ovid, Post Office of Ovid.

United States, War Department. *The War of the Rebellion.* Series 1, 53 vols. Washington, D.C.: Government Printing Office, 1880–98.

Washington, D.C. National Archives:
Record Group 49, "Records of the Bureau of Land Management. Records Relating to Public Land Disposals ca. 1796–1951 with a few dated as early as 1770." Patents Received Under the Desert Land Act of March 3, 1877. Xerographic copies of Winfield Scott's patent and several in his general vicinity on file in the Scottsdale Public Library.

Record Group 94, "Records of the Adjutant General's Office 1780s–1917. Records of the Record and Pension Office, 1784–1917." Civil War, Pension and A.C.P. Files of Winfield Scott. Xerographic copies on file in the Scottsdale Public Library.

State and Territorial

Arizona. Department of Library, Archives and Public Records: Corporation Commission, Incorporating Division, Book 17 (May 12 to July 22, 1902). Articles of Incorporation of the Coast Line Copper Company.

Corporation Commission, Incorporating Division, Dead Files. Articles of Association of the Orange Belt and Scottsdale Railroad Company.

Corporation Commission, Incorporating Division, Dead Files. Articles of Incorporation of the Socorro Gold Mining Company.

Maricopa County Superior Court, Probate Division. Case 1571, Winfield Scott.

Journals of the Twentieth Legislative Assembly of the Territory of Arizona. Phoenix: Press of J. O. Dunbar, 1899.

Journals of the Twenty-fifth Legislative Assembly of the Territory of Arizona. Phoenix: Press of Phoenix Printing Co., 1909.

Local

Maricopa County, Arizona. Board of Supervisors. Minutes of the Board of Supervisors, Office Book 5.

Maricopa County, Arizona. Recorder's Office:
Warranty Deed Books.
Subdivision Plat Maps.

Oakland County, Michigan. Clerk's Office. Deed Books. Photostatic copies of Scott family deeds forwarded by Lynn D. Allen, County Clerk. Copies on file in the Scottsdale Public Library.

San Bernardino County, California. Recorder's Office. Deed Books. Photostatic copy of Winfield Scott's homestead filing forwarded by V. Dennis Wardle, County Recorder. Copy on file in the Scottsdale Public Library.

City Directories

A. P. Skinner's Phoenix City Directory, 1903. Phoenix: A. P. Skinner, n.d.

A. P. Skinner's Phoenix City and Maricopa County Directory (Arizona), 1905–6. Phoenix: A. P. Skinner, n.d.

Arizona Business Directory, 1907–1908. Denver: Gazetteer Publishing Co., 1907.

Arizona Business Directory, 1909–1910. Denver: Gazetteer Publishing Co., 1909.

The Bensel Directory Co.'s Phoenix Directory for the Year 1892. n.d. Reprint. Phoenix: Paul Johnson Jewelers, 1971.

Langley's San Francisco Directory. San Francisco: Francis, Valentine and Co., 1881.

Meyer's Business Directory of the City of Phoenix, Arizona. Phoenix: A. Leonard Meyer, 1888.

The Phoenix Directory Co.'s City Directory for the Year 1897. Phoenix: Phoenix Directory Co., n.d.

Phoenix Directory Co.'s Phoenix Directory for 1899–1900. Phoenix: Phoenix Directory Co., 1899–1900.

The San Francisco Directory. San Francisco: Francis, Valentine and Co., 1879.

Newspapers

Alta California (San Francisco) 1878–1880.

Arizona Gazette (Phoenix) 1894–1897 and selected issues in 1885, 1889, 1893, 1898, 1901–1906, 1908, 1910–1911.

Arizona Journal-Miner (Prescott) 1899–1900.

Arizona Republican (Phoenix) 1897–1911 and selected issues in 1890–1891, 1893, 1895–1896.

Arizona Star (Tucson) selected issues in 1891, 1895, 1898–1899, 1902–1903.

Astorian (Astoria, Oregon) 1882–1885.

Evangel (San Francisco) 1875–1879.

Leavenworth Times 1865–1871.

Los Angeles Star 1876–1878.

Nevada State Journal (Reno) 1881–1882.

Phoenix Herald 1888–1899 and selected issues in 1883.

Prescott Courier selected issues in 1899, 1901–1902, 1904.

Reno Gazette 1881–1882.

Rocky Mountain News (Denver) Photocopies of articles containing references to Winfield Scott, 1871–1874, supplied by the Western History Department, Denver Public Library.

Saturday Evening Press (Phoenix) 1897–1898.

Scott's TOWN BULL O'Tin (Scottsdale) May, 1922.

Syracuse Journal Photocopies of articles containing references to Winfield Scott, 1861–1863, supplied by the Onandaga Historical Association, Syracuse, New York.

Tempe News selected issues in 1890, 1897–1899, 1901, 1903–1904.
Tucson Citizen selected issues in 1902, 1904.

Autobiographies and Memoirs

Stimson, H. K. *From the Stage Coach to the Pulpit.* Edited by T. W. Greene. St. Louis: R. A. Campbell, 1874.

Summerhayes, Martha. *Vanished Arizona.* 4th ed. Tucson: Arizona Silhouettes, 1960.

Interviews

Mrs. Ethel Hayden Evans. February 26, 1977.

Mrs. Murle Miller Foley. March 1, 1977, and June 16, 1977.

Mrs. Veronica Dorris Greene. February 28, 1977.

Mrs. May Vanderhoof Mathis. July 29, 1974.

Mrs. Elsie Elliott Severance. May 9, 10, 11, 1975, and December 19, 20, 21, 1976.

Mr. George F. Spaulding. May 12, 1975.

Miss Marjorie Thomas. August 9, 1974; March 26, 1975; and May 8, 1975.

Unpublished Material

Scott, Winfield. "Pickett's Charge As Seen from the Front Line." A Paper Prepared and Read before California Commandery of the Military Order of the Loyal Legion of the United States. February 8, 1888.

"S.H.S. '23" Scottsdale High School Yearbook. Mimeographed. Scottsdale, Ariz.: Scottsdale High School, 1923.

Typescripts

Mrs. Minnie Scott Albright. January 3, 1953.

Mrs. Bertha Blount McFarland. July 13, 1940.

Mrs. Helen Hayden Meeker. September 15, 1975.

Mrs. Elsie Elliott Severance. January 1, 1975, and April 21, 1975.

Mr. George F. Spaulding. 1972.

SECONDARY SOURCES

Periodical Articles

Barney, James M. "The Early Annals of Scottsdale." *The Sheriff Magazine* 13 (June, 1954):53 and 55.

"A Big Failure" [Arizona Improvement Company] *Irrigation Age* 12 (December, 1897):76.

"A City Built in an Orange Grove-Ingleside" [advertisement]. *The Border* 1 (November, 1909):facing p.16.

Fels, Rendigs. "American Business Cycles, 1865–79." *American Economic Review* 41 (June, 1951):325–49.

[Freeman D. Rickerson]. *Baptist Home Mission Monthly* 12 (October, 1890):312.

"A Gain-But at a Loss" [Freeman D. Rickerson]. *Baptist Home Mission Monthly* 14 (May, 1892):156–57.

Lounsbury, Thomas R. "In the Defenses of Washington." *Yale Review* n.s. 2 (April, 1913):385–411.

Smith, David C. "Middle Range Farming in the Civil War Era: Life on a Farm in Seneca County, 1862–1866." *New York History* 48 (October, 1967):352–369.

Smith, Richard K. "For God, For Country, For the Territory." *Arizona Highways* 49 (April, 1973):6–13.

Tait, Magnus. "Fruit Growing in Arizona." *Rural Californian* 18 (January, 1895):30.

Taylor, David G. "Boom Town Leavenworth: The Failure of the Dream." *The Kansas Historical Quarterly* 38 (Winter, 1972):389–415.

Young, Etta Gifford. "Ingleside, Scottsdale and Environs." *Arizona* 4 (June, 1914):4–5, 9.

Books and Pamphlets

Andreas, Alfred T. *History of the State of Kansas*. Chicago: A. T. Andreas, 1883.

Angel, Myron, ed. *History of Nevada*. Oakland: Thompson and West, 1881.

Bancroft, Hubert Howe. *History of Arizona and New Mexico, 1530–1888*. San Francisco: History Co., 1889.

——————. *History of California, 1860–1890*. San Francisco: History Co., 1890.

Barnes, Will C. *Arizona Place Names*. rev. and enl. by Byrd H. Granger. Tucson: University of Arizona Press, 1960.

The Bay of San Francisco. 2 vols. Chicago: Lewis Publishing Co., 1892.

Beck, Warren A., and Williams, David A. *California*. Garden City, N.Y.: Doubleday and Co., 1972.

Bedini, Silvio A. *Ridgefield in Review*. Ridgefield, Conn.: Ridgefield 250th Anniversary Committee, 1958.

Bryan, Leslie A., ed. *Bassett's Notes on Coverts*. Champaign, Ill., 1957.

Carnahan, J. Worth. *Manual of the Civil War and Key to the Grand Army of the Republic and Kindred Societies*. rev. ed. Washington, D.C.: U.S. Army and Navy Historical Association, 1899.

Cathcart, William, ed. *The Baptist Encyclopedia*. Philadelphia: Louis H. Everts, 1881.

Catton, Bruce. *Mr. Lincoln's Army*. Garden City, N.Y.: Doubleday and Co., 1951.

——————. *The Glory Road*. Garden City, N.Y.: Doubleday and Co., 1952.

——————. *A Stillness at Appomattox*. Garden City, N.Y.: Doubleday and Co., 1953.

——————. *This Hallowed Ground*. Garden City, N.Y.: Doubleday and Co., 1956.

——————. *Terrible Swift Sword*. Garden City, N.Y.: Doubleday and Co., 1963.

——————. *Never Call Retreat*. Garden City, N.Y.: Doubleday and Co., 1965.

Caughey, John W. *California*. 3d ed. Englewood Cliffs, N.J.: Prentice-Hall, 1970.

Cleland, Robert Glass. *A History of Phelps Dodge, 1834–1950*. New York: Alfred A. Knopf, 1952.

Christy, Lloyd B. *Life History of Col. William Christy*. Facts of publication not given.

Colorado Baptist Annual, 1873. Kansas City: Allen and Ward, 1873.

Colorado Baptist Annual, A.D. 1874. Kansas City: Allen and Ward, 1874.

Colorado Baptist Annual, A.D. 1875. Philadelphia: J. A. Wagenseller, 1875.

Colorado Baptist Annual, A.D. 1876. Philadelphia: J. A. Wagenseller, 1876.

Companions of the Military Order of the Loyal Legion of the United States. New York: L. R. Hamersly Co., 1901.

Connors, Jo, comp. *Who's Who in Arizona*. Tucson: Jo Connors, 1913.

Davis, Samuel P., ed. *The History of Nevada*. 2 vols. Los Angeles: Elms Publishing Co., 1913.

Dictionary of American Biography. rev. ed. s.v. "Lounsbury, Thomas Raynesford."

Durant, Samuel W. *History of Oakland County, Michigan*. Philadelphia: L. H. Everts and Co., 1877.

Dyer, Frederick Henry. *A Compendium of the War of the Rebellion*. 1908. Reprint (1 vol in 3) New York: Thomas Yoseloff, 1959.

Federal Writers' Project. *Colorado*. New York: Hastings House, 1941.

——————. *Kansas*. New York: Viking Press, 1939.

——————. *Oregon*. Portland, Oreg.: Binfords and Mort, 1940.

——————. *Washington*. Portland, Oreg.: Binfords and Mort, 1941.

Fleming, Sanford. *For the Making of Ministers*. Valley Forge, Pa.: Judson Press, 1963.

Frazer, Robert W. *Forts of the West*. Norman: University of Oklahoma Press, 1965.

Gregory, Thomas Jefferson. *History of Yolo County, California*. Los Angeles: Historic Record Co., 1913.

Gudde, Erwin G. *California Place Names*. 2d ed. Berkeley and Los Angeles: University of California Press, 1960.

Guinn, James Miller. *History of the State of California and Biographical Record of the Sacramento Valley, California*. Chicago: Chapman Publishing Co., 1906.

——————. *A History of California and an Extended History of Los Angeles and Environs*. 3 vols. Los Angeles: Historic Record Co., 1915.

Halsey, Lewis. *History of the Seneca Baptist Association*. Ithaca: Journal Association Book and Job Printing House, 1879.

Handy, Robert T., ed. *The Social Gospel in America, 1870–1920*. New York: Oxford University Press, 1966.

Hibbard, Benjamin Horace. *A History of the Public Land Policies*. 1924. Reprint. New York: Peter Smith, 1939.

A Historical and Biographical Record of the Territory of Arizona. Chicago: McFarland and Poole, 1896.

History of San Bernardino County, California. 1883. Reprint. Riverside, Calif.: Riverside Museum Press, 1965.

Hopkins, Charles Howard. *The Rise of the Social Gospel in American Protestantism, 1865–1915*. New Haven: Yale University Press, 1940.

Hopkins, Ernest J., and Thomas, Alfred, Jr. *The Arizona State University Story*. Phoenix: Southwest Publishing Co., 1960.

Hughes, Tom. *History of Banning and San Gorgonio Pass*. Banning, Calif.: Banning Record Printers, ca. 1938.

Jackson, W. Turrentine. *Wagon Roads West*. Berkeley and Los Angeles: University of California Press, 1952.

Kemper, Clarence W. *The Story of "Old First."* Denver, 1938.

Lothrop, W. C. *Historical Sketch of the Sunday School, First Baptist Church, Denver, Colorado*. Denver: Tribune Printing House, 1876.

Lutrell, Estelle. *Newspapers and Periodicals of Arizona, 1859–1911*. University of Arizona Bulletin, General Bulletin no. 15. Tucson: University of Arizona Press, 1950.

Marberry, M. M. *The Golden Voice*. New York: Farrar, Straus and Co., 1947.

McClintock, James H. *Arizona*. 3 vols. Chicago: S. J. Clarke Publishing Co., 1891.

A Memorial and Biographical History of Northern California. Chicago: Lewis Publishing Co., 1891.

Miers, Earl Schenck, ed. *Lincoln Day by Day*. 3 vols. Washington, D.C.: Lincoln Sesquicentennial Commission, 1960.

Minutes of the Eleventh Annual Meeting of the Kansas Baptist Convention. Topeka: Commonwealth State Printing House Book Rooms, 1870.

Minutes of the Twelfth Annual Meeting of the Kansas Baptist Convention. Ottawa, Kan.: *Ottowa Herald,* 1871.

Morison, Samuel Eliot, and Commager, Henry Steele. *The Growth of the American Republic.* 2 vols. 5th ed., rev. and enl. New York: Oxford University Press, 1962.

Murphy, Merwin L. *W. J. and the Valley.* Alhambra, Calif.: Merwin L. Murphy, 1975.

Myrick, David F. *Railroads of Arizona.* Vol. 1. Berkeley: Howell–North Books, 1975.

New York Monuments Commission for the Battlefields of Gettysburg and Chattanooga. *Final Report on the Battlefield of Gettysburg.* 3 vols. Albany: J. B. Lyon Co., 1902.

Peplow, Edward H., Jr. *History of Arizona.* 3 vols. New York: Lewis Historical Publishing Co., 1958.

Phisterer, Frederick, comp. *New York in the War of the Rebellion, 1861 to 1865.* 6 vols. 3d ed. Albany: J. B. Lyon Co., 1912.

Portrait and Biographical Record of Arizona. Chicago: Chapman Publishing Co., 1901.

Powell, William H. *Records of Living Officers of the United States Army.* Philadelphia: L. R. Hamersly and Co., 1890.

Prucha, Francis Paul. *A Guide to the Military Posts of the United States.* Madison: State Historical Society of Wisconsin, 1964.

Robbins, Roy M. *Our Landed Heritage.* 1942. Reprint. Gloucester, Mass.: Peter Smith, 1960.

Rolle, Andrew F. *California.* 2d ed. New York: Thomas Y. Crowell Co., 1969.

Rydjord, John. *Kansas Place Names.* Norman: University of Oklahoma Press, 1972.

Scott, Mrs. Winfield. *Half Mast and Other Poems.* Facts of publication not given.

Shadegg, Stephen C. *Century One.* Phoenix: W. A. Krueger, 1969.

Sloan, Richard E., ed. *History of Arizona.* 4 vols. Phoenix: Record Publishing Co., 1930.

Smiley, Jerome C., ed. *History of Denver.* 1901. Reprint. Denver: Colorado State Historical Society, 1971.

Sonnichsen, C. L. *Colonel Greene and the Copper Skyrocket.* Tucson: University of Arizona Press, 1974.

Stevens, Maud. *A Century of Baptist Faith, 1864–1964.* Denver: First Baptist Church of Denver, Colorado, 1963.

Stover, Earl F. *Up from Handymen - The U.S. Army Chaplaincy, 1865–1920.* Washington, D.C.: Office of the Chief of Chaplains, Department of the Army, 1977.

Sullivan, James, ed. *History of New York State.* 5 vols. New York: Lewis Historical Publishing Co., 1927.

Teller, Daniel Webster. *The History of Ridgefield Connecticut.* Danbury, Conn.: T. Donovan, 1878.

Thrapp, Dan L. *The Conquest of Apacheria.* Norman: University of Oklahoma Press, 1967.

Vickers, W. B. *History of the City of Denver, Arapahoe County, and Colorado.* Chicago: O. L. Baskin and Co., 1880.

Wagoner, Jay J. *Arizona Territory, 1863–1912.* Tucson: University of Arizona Press, 1970.

Walker, Henry Pickering. *The Wagonmasters.* Norman: University of Oklahoma Press, 1966.

Warren, George F., and Pearson, Frank A. *Prices.* New York: John Wiley and Sons, 1933.

Whiting, J. S. *Forts of the State of Washington*. 2d ed. Seattle: J. S. Whiting, 1951.

Whittemore, Margaret. *Historic Kansas*. Lawrence: University of Kansas Press, 1954.

Willson, Arabella M. *Disaster, Struggle, Triumph*. Albany: Argus Co., 1870.

Wolle, Muriel Sibell. *Stampede to Timberline*. Boulder, Colo.: Muriel S. Wolle, 1949.

Wren, Thomas, ed. *A History of the State of Nevada*. New York: Lewis Publishing Co., 1904.

Zornow, William Frank. *Kansas*. Norman: University of Oklahoma Press, 1957.

Theses, Dissertations, and Unpublished Studies

Blunt, Bruce Keith. "Ninety Years of Baptist Missionary Administration in Colorado." Th.D. dissertation, Central Baptist Theological Seminary, 1951.

Cooley, Doris E. "History of the First Baptist Church, Leavenworth, Kansas." Mimeographed. Leavenworth, Kans.: Doris E. Cooley, ca. 1959.

Dick, Wilburn W. "The History of the Scottsdale School System at Scottsdale, Arizona, 1896–1944." Master's thesis, Arizona State Teachers College, 1944.

Henderson, Patrick C. "The Public Domain in Arizona: 1863–1891." Ph.D. dissertation, University of New Mexico, 1965.

Jeffrey, Robert S. "The History of Douglas, Arizona." Master's thesis, University of Arizona, 1952.

Wright, DeForeest B. "The Story of Winfield Scott." Typescript. Hollywood, Calif.: DeForeest B. Wright, 1970.

Index